A BIRDWATCHER'S MISCELLANY

A BIRDWATCHER'S MISCELLANY

EDITED BY ROB HUME

BLANDFORD PRESS
POOLE . DORSET

First published in the UK 1984 by Blandford Press,
Link House, West Street, Poole, Dorset, BH15 1LL

Distributed in the United States by
Sterling Publishing Co., Inc.,
2 Park Avenue, New York, N.Y. 10016

British Library Cataloguing in Publication Data

A Birdwatcher's miscellany.
  1. Birds
  I. Hume, Rob
  598   QL673

  ISBN 0-7137-1385-2

Typeset by Graphicraft Typesetters Ltd., Hong Kong

Printed in Great Britain by
Biddles Ltd, Guildford, Surrey

CONTENTS

FOREWORD BY BILL ODDIE

Not long ago I was asked to fill in a questionnaire about my reading habits. It was sent to me by a perplexed but enterprising English teacher, and it included questions like: 'Do you read regularly?', 'How many books do you read each year?', 'What is your favourite novel?', 'Which author do you most admire?', and so on and so forth. The teacher had apparently sent the same questionnaire to several other so-called 'celebrities'. His idea was that he would show our answers to his uppity pupils who, on realizing that their 'heroes' (me!?) were steeped in the joys of fine literature would be provoked into *reading* their set books instead of making them into paper darts.

'See here kids,' he could say, 'Bill Oddie says he owes everything to John Milton, and he read *War & Peace again* yesterday – twice!'

'And look where its got *him!*' the uppity pupils might reply. 'Prancing around doing silly T.V. shows, and writing forewords for bird books!'

Now I don't want to encourage uppity pupils, but they'd be right. As a matter of fact I did study English Literature at Cambridge – I'm an M.A. cantab no less! – and indeed I have read *Paradise Lost* – and *Regained* – and *War & Peace* (only once mind you) and, to be honest, I was bored stiff by the lot of them. By the end of my University career I'd come to a disturbing conclusion: I didn't really like books! And the fact is, doing English at Cambridge almost put me off reading for life! This is surely sad, as I dare say many of the great works of English

Literature are not only very enlightening and very instructive but may well be very enjoyable too. I shall never know, because unfortunately many of them are also very long. Which is something else that puts me off. I can tell if I'll enjoy reading a book by weighing it in my hand or counting the pages. Anything over two ounces, or 150 pages, is insurmountable, especially if it hasn't got pictures.

I did, of course, sympathise with the teacher, so I didn't fill in the questionnaire. If I had done I don't think it would have helped his case one little bit, and I rather doubt that he would have understood my answers anyway, unless he is a jazz fan or a birdwatcher. The truth is, the only publications I regularly read (and totally devour) are *Down Beat*, *Black Music* and *British Birds*! And if no other words ever rolled off the world's printing presses it wouldn't really bother me much. I do *possess* quite a lot of books, and it might have impressed the teacher to know I bought well over twenty last year, but they are *all* bird books, and would it really have inspired his uppity pupils had I listed my 'favourite author' as 'Sharrock, Willis and Ferguson-Lees', or the hundred and odd contributors to the *British Birds* Rare Birds Issue!? I exempt bird books from my generally philistine dismissal of reading because for a start there aren't that many of them you really have to *read* – you can 'skim through' a field guide, or 'flick through' a book of photos, or 'dip into' a miscellany.

Which of course brings me to this particular collection. This is my kind of book. It has an awful lot going for it. Firstly, every word is about birds. Secondly, because it's a *collection*, I don't have to read it all at once. Thirdly, it includes all the 'good bits' from many other books that I'd no doubt enjoy very much but won't read because they weigh more than two ounces. Fourthly, it is excellent value, as for the price of *one* book you purchase the essential parts of nearly fifty (all of which I can now authoritatively quote as if I've read them entirely!). And lastly, and best of all, there is amongst the many extracts not a single line from *Paradise Lost* or *War & Peace* (and, to make it even classier, there's nothing from any of my books in here either).

Oh, there is one serious flaw – you might well get so absorbed you'll forget to go out birdwatching. Risk it. Read on and enjoy.

Bill Oddie

ACKNOWLEDGEMENTS

Every effort has been made to trace the copyright-holders of all the material included in this book. The publishers would like to thank the authors and publishers of those books listed in the Bibliography for permission to reproduce passages of text. In addition, thanks are due to the following artists and publishers for permission to reproduce line drawings.

Robert Gillmor: pp. 17, 23, 27, 34, 52, 57, 75, 84, 87, 89, 146, 165.
J.M. Dent & Sons Ltd (*Natural History of British Birds*, Eric Simms): pp. 38, 44, 155, 179.
British Trust for Ornithology/T. and A.D. Poyser Ltd (*Atlas of Breeding Birds of Britain and Ireland*): pp. 61, 70, 151.
Donald Watson/T. and A.D. Poyser Ltd (*The Hen Harrier*, Donald Watson, and *The Peregrine Falcon*, D. Ratcliffe): pp. 116, 124.
John Busby/T. and A.D. Poyser Ltd (*The Gannet*): p. 64.
Laurel Tucker: p. 129.
Killian Mullarney: p. 185.
Richard Millington: p. 169.
* Fair Isle Bird Observatory Trust: p. 79 and title page.

The drawing on p. 161 by C.F. Tunnicliffe was first published in *Bird Portraiture*, The Studio 1945. Those on pp. 14, 19, 32, 72, 93, 113, 119, 127, 153, 175, 183 were originally published in *A Manual of British Birds*, Gurney and Jackson 1889. Those on pp. 31, 48, 82, 101, 106, 111, 134, 141, 144, 150, 158, 171 are by the author.

* The Fair Isle Bird Observatory Trust operates an Observatory on Fair Isle (Shetlands) with accommodation for 24 people. Since 1948, the Trust has made a continuous study of bird migration movements and has recently undertaken research into the habits of seabirds. For further datails, contact the Secretary, Fair Isle Bird Observatory Trust, 21 Regent Terrace, Edinburgh EH7 5BT.

INTRODUCTION

What is birdwatching all about? What should birdwatchers attempt to achieve? Julian Huxley (*Bird-watching and Bird Behaviour*, 1950) gives some answers.

An appreciable part of the feelings which you have for a countryside will, if you are a bird-watcher, be derived from its birds. An American landscape may now and again look surprisingly like an English one; but its birds will speedily remind you of its alien character. The blue-jays and American robins, thrushes and cat-birds, chipping sparrows and vireos – what a different quality they give from our English blackbirds and rooks, thrushes, redbreasts and wagtails, chaffinches and white-throats.

The bird-watcher by his knowledge of birds' notes may come by experiences from which others are debarred. One early morning towards the close of last year, I was lying in bed, just awake, on the shores of the Victoria Nyanza, close on the equator in Central Africa. From my window, I could see the fronds of a tall palm-tree. At its foot, though the season was December, there were bright flower-beds and green lawns; and beyond there was a park-like stretch of grass, dotted with magnificent trees all in leaf, sloping down to the soft blue waters of the lake under the bright sun. Suddenly a song came from just outside the window – the song of a willow wren, a willow wren on migration three or four thousand miles from the place where it was hatched; and automatically, as I heard the fresh and delicate dying fall of the notes, they brought back to me all the other attributes and associations which give the willow wren its particular character – the slender, modest,

9

green-brown body of the singer, the cool of an English spring, a piece of rough furzeland, with the leaves barely unfolded on the birch-trees, the bird prying about for the few early insects. The willow wren is the antithesis of all that is tropical, an embodiment of freshness, delicacy and northern springtime; it was strange and even moving to hear it thus in the heart of Africa.

In the same sort of way the yellow-hammer's song seems the best possible expression of hot country roads in July, the turtle-dove's crooning of midsummer afternoons, the redshank's call of seabreeze over saltings and tidal mudflats, the robin's song of peaceful autumnal melancholy as the leaves fall in a sun which has lost its warming power.

The bird-watcher watches because he loves watching, because birds are good to look at, because their characters and doings interest him.

Birdwatching, of course, can mean many different things to different people. That is part of its appeal; one can make almost anything of it. It can be simply a summer-weekend recreation – a pleasant diversion to be dipped into from time to time whenever a suitable free moment presents itself. It is increasingly looked upon as a sport. It can, of course, be a science. Either way it can become obsessive. What characterises the birdwatchers whose writings are sampled in the present book, and the birdwatcher, like myself, who counts birds as his major lifelong interest, is not just that birds are an obsession. Indeed, they are not even quite that – the sort of obsession which lasts a short time then burns itself out. Neither are they simply things to be watched every weekend in a burst of frenzied enthusiasm which is turned off in between times. They actually become a way of life.

Bird books are read assiduously, birds are watched on television, studied in magazines, the subject of paintings on the wall, recordings, photographs and endless pages of notes – but, chiefly, they are always there. Julian Huxley, in the piece quoted above, had to make no conscious effort, no kind of preparation to enjoy the willow warbler and all the thoughts which it stimulated within him. He could not switch it on, or decide to hear it at a particular moment. Enjoying birds to the full is not a matter of going out for three hours every weekend, like going to a football match, and forgetting them in the meantime. It is a case of being aware of them at all times, able to react immediately, unconsciously, should a bird make its presence known – an appreciation of something outside man's world and control, living its own life, but capable of a powerful influence on his imagination and aesthetic senses.

On top of this comes the desire to understand, study, or simply identify birds. It is all a development of the enjoyment and love of birds which is surely the basis on which all good birdwatchers build. It brings excitement, satisfaction, disappointment, puzzlement and frustration. Anyone who has waited hours for a glimpse of an exciting new rarity (especially when everyone else has already seen it without trouble), or who has unexpectedly discovered one for himself, will confirm that anger, despair and almost uncontrollable elation are not words too strong to describe what birdwatching can be like either! There is a tremendously strong emotional response sometimes; bird-watching brings great highs and sometimes deep lows to the committed birdwatcher, which those who have never tasted it and have no wish to think deeply about it will never appreciate. The highs may come from a very common bird, in an unusual situation or a particularly beautiful setting, as much as from the rare ones.

The extracts quoted in this book are offered as an attempt to convey some of the kinds of pleasurable experiences which birdwatching offers. The object has not been simply to go for the purple prose. In a period in which picture books, field guides and weighty, technical volumes dominate ornithological publishing, however, I have been prompted to select things which, above all, are a good read. The whole object of the book is to supply just that – but I think it also shows that it is possible to write well and attractively whilst giving accurate and valuable information. It is a plea, if you like, for good, readable bird books. Some of the modern works quoted do show that top quality, scientifically correct and important material can, indeed, be written in an exciting and imaginative manner.

It is not just a collection of old writings. Many of the books used are out of print (it has been partly my aim to sample writing not now easily available) but much is of fairly recent date. Many well-known authors are missing. This is not to be taken to mean that I have a low opinion of them. Mainly it is because they have appeared in anthologies often enough before, or their books are still easy to find or have been recently reprinted.

The fact that I tried to make a selection of writings which I found informative and good to read inevitably, perhaps, led me to produce an initial draft twice as long as that required. It has been a pity to see so much go – but I must thank the editors, particularly Alison Copland, for cutting it down to size! I hope that you, the reader, find the result successful, both entertaining and profitable to read.

1 FAMILIAR BIRDS

Familiar birds in familiar places attract little attention from the average birdwatcher, and their beauty is often taken for granted or overlooked entirely. Derek Goodwin in *Birds of Man's World* (1978) helps to put that right with these observations on the pheasant.

The Pheasant is often wrongly spoken of as "pampered" by those who disapprove of game-preserving; it is in fact a very tough and viable bird and the oft-repeated statement that it would "die out" but for game-preservation is almost certainly untrue. Or perhaps I had better say it is only true of those areas, and they are all too many, where it is in fact, if not in theory, persecuted by man in season and out. So long as man does not prey too heavily on it the wild, or feral, Pheasant manages to maintain its numbers in many areas. It likes plenty of cover and although often in quite dry woods shows some preference for low-lying, rather wet woods, the tangled scrub along stream banks, reedbeds and similar places. However, it feeds a lot in fields, glades in woods and other open areas and can often make do with surprisingly little cover. It is omnivorous, taking largely vegetable food such as seeds, shoots, and buds of many plants, chestnuts, acorns, and berries. It also takes some insects and the young chicks feed chiefly on insects at first although they quite soon begin to take some vegetable food.

In the few places where it is not shot at the Pheasant soon becomes relatively indifferent to people, if it constantly sees them, and then becomes a living ornament whose beauty can be appreciated by the ordinary passer-by as well as by the bird-watcher with binoculars. I seldom see a cock Pheasant, shining in the sun, without thinking of the ancient Greek philosopher, Solon, who, when asked by the vainglorious Persian king if he (Solon) had ever seen anything so magnificent as himself and his court replied that, having seen the beauty of the Pheasant, he could no longer be impressed by mere human finery.

Appreciating such beauty is part of the general attraction of birdwatching, but getting to know individual birds intimately is a particular aspect of bird study which is not practised by most modern birdwatchers. The rewards, however, can be immense – as Len Howard found and described in her book *Birds as Individuals* (1952). The following two extracts serve to illustrate the observation and intelligent interpretation of her subjects, in this case great tits.

It seems evident that birds can communicate with each other by slight inflections of voice and of movement, because I find those that know me well understand much by their sensitive interpretation of my voice or least movement. For example, when Great Tits want to peck at my butter dish, which they know is usually forbidden, they perch a little way off and look first at the butter, then at my face, hesitating although

Great tit – instantly recognisable from this woodcut.

longing to help themselves, for they have a passion for butter. If I say "come on" coaxingly, they confidently step up and eat it. If I say "no" just a little sternly they remain where they are, but continue to look pleadingly at me and then at the butter. A shade crosser "no" sends them hopping farther off; an angry "no" makes them fly to the open window, but if I quickly call out, "Here, come on," in a very coaxing tone, they at once return and if I keep quiet, inch by inch they hop along the table towards the butter, still eyeing me for further signs of objection. Once on their guard by "no" in the first place, they will not step up with the airy confidence shown when I encourage them by saying "Come on" at first. They interpret correctly any sign of objection in voice or movement, but without the encouraging tone of voice they will not touch butter while I am looking because I have once or twice forbidden them by an angry "no". Their extreme sensitiveness makes them learn extraordinarily quickly. I have to know the bird before communicating satisfactorily by voice inflection; strangers are naturally uncertain through nervousness, but Great Tits generally learn my meaning very soon.

The second extract concerns an individual great tit, which she had named Baldhead.

In personal intercourse with Baldhead I am sometimes outwitted. His favourite food is nuts and last autumn I brought some indoors in a paper bag, giving him one which he ate on the rungs under a chair. Knowing he would tear open the bag to help himself to another, I wrapped it in a double-folded teacloth, rolling this round the bag and turning both ends under securely in a way that seemed impossible for a small bird to undo. I placed this on a side-table. I had my back to Baldhead while wrapping the bag and he could not possibly have seen what I was doing from where he was, under the chair seat. He soon flew to my hand for more nut, but I gave him cheese – his second choice of food. He threw this away with an impatient toss and looked up at me expectantly. Again I offered him cheese. He made a curious sort of grimace with his beak half-opened, refused to take the cheese and flew round the room, looking for but unable to find the paper bag. I left the room for a few minutes; on my return he flew out of the fanlight window with the haste habitual to him after theft. Several nuts were rolling on the side-table. He had pulled the cloth undone and torn open the paper bag, helping himself to a nut. I had never before wrapped food in this cloth or in any other kind of cloth, nor had I ever put bird food on that side-table, which was used for painting materials, so he had no reason to suspect the cloth contained the paper bag, which was solidly covered with a double layer of cloth.

An earlier writer, Edmund Selous, was a tremendous bird watcher. He really did *watch* birds, not simply giving them a superficial glance but using his powers of observation and enquiry to the full. In *Bird Life Glimpses* (1905) he describes moments of excitement as dawn breaks over a heronry in Suffolk.

There is a heronry on an estate here, into which, in the early spring, I have sometimes crept, coming before dawn, in silence and darkness, to be there when it awoke. What an awakening! A sudden scream, as though the night were stabbed, and cried out - a scream to chill one's very blood - followed by a deep "oogh," and then a most extraordinary noise in the throat, a kind of croak sometimes, but more often a kind of pipe, like a subdued siren - a fog-signal - yet pleasing, even musical. Sometimes, again, it suggests the tones of the human voice - weirdly, eerily - vividly caught for a moment, then an Ovid's metamorphosis. This curious sound, in the production of which the neck is as the long tube of some metal instrument, is very characteristic, and constantly heard. And now scream after scream, each one more harsh and wild than the last, rings out from tree to tree. Other sounds - strange, wild, grotesque - cannot even suffer an attempt to describe them. All this through the darkness, the black of which is now beginning to be "dipped in grey." There is the snapping of the bill, too - a soft click, a musical "pip, pip" - amidst all these uncouth noises. On the whole, it is the grotesque in sound - a carnival of hoarse, wild, grotesque inarticulations. Amidst them, every now and then, one hears the great sweep of pinions, and a shadowy form, just thickening on the gloom, is lost in the profounder gloom of some tree that receives it.

Most of the nests are in sad, drooping-boughed firs - spruces, a name that suits them not - trees whose very branches are a midnight, as Longfellow has called them, in a great, though seldom-mentioned poem. Others are in grand old beeches, which, with the slender white birch and the maple, stand in open clearings amidst the shaggy firs, and make this plantation a paradise. Sometimes, as the herons fly out of one tree into another, they make a loud, sonorous beating with their great wings, whilst at others, they glide with long, silent-sounding swishes, that seem a part of the darkness. Two will, often, pursue each other, with harshest screams, and, all at once, from one of them comes a shout of wild, maniacal laughter, that sets the blood a-tingling, and makes one a better man to hear. Whilst sweeping, thus, in nuptial flight, about their nesting-trees, they stretch out their long necks in front of them, sometimes quite straight, more often bent near the breast like a crooked piece of copper wire. A strange appearance! – everything stiff and abrupt, odd-looking, uncouth, no graceful curves or sweeps. The long legs, carried horizontally, balance the neck behind – but grotesquely, as one gargoyle glares at another. Thus herons fly within the heronry, but as they sail out, *en voyage*, the head is drawn back between the shoulders, in the more familiar way. As morning dawns, the shadowy "air-drawn" forms begin to appear more substantially. Several of the birds may then be seen perched about in the trees, some gaunt and upright, others hunched up in a heap, with, perhaps, one

Grey heron – about to strike after a long, patient wait.

statuesque figure placed, like a sentinel, on the top of a tall, slender larch, the thin pinnacle of the trunk of which is bent over to form a perch.

Other, and much sweeter, sounds begin now to mingle with the harsh, though not unpleasing screams, and, increasing every moment in volume, make them, at last, but part of a universal and most divine harmony. The whole plantation has become a song. Song-thrush and mistle-thrush make it up, mostly, between them, but all help, and all is a music; chatters and twitters seem glorified, nothing sounds harshly, joy makes it melody. There is a time – the daylight of dawn, but not daylight – when the birds sing everywhere, as though to salute it. As the real daylight comes, this sinks and almost ceases, and never in the whole twenty-four hours, is there such an hour again. The laugh, and answering laugh, of the green woodpecker is frequent, now, and mingles sweetly with the loud cooing of the wood-pigeons – not the characteristic note, but another, very much like that of dovecot pigeons, when they make a few quick little turns from one side to another, moving the feet dancingly, but keeping almost in the same place: a brisk, satisfied sound, not the pompous rolling coo of a serious proposal, nor yet that more tender-meaning note, with which the male broods on the nest, caressed by the female. But the representative of this last, in the wood-pigeon – the familiar spring and summer sound – is now frequently heard, and seems getting towards perfection. So, at last, it is day, and the loud, bold clarion of the pheasant is like the rising sun.

The sheer delight exhibited in this piece at an encounter with familiar birds is not shared by all ornithological writers! Kelsall and Munn (*The Birds of Hampshire and the Isle of Wight*, 1905) were less than complimentary about the house sparrow.

It is the happy privilege of those who live in the New Forest to be able to walk for a whole day without seeing this bird, but in order to perform the feat they must not start from a railway station.

Most people, however, are most appreciative of the common birds found in a familiar English country lane. G. K. Yeates (*A Bird Lover's Britain*, 1937) describes the scene.

Late March and April soon sets the hedges alive with nesting birds. First in the field the song thrush builds his model nest soon to contain those eggs of blue which year in, year out, never fail to prove more decisively than any other fact that spring has really come. Indeed in all the whole range of bird life the aesthetic sense will never be more satisfactorily gratified than in the vision of those blue eggs. Their tight-sitting owner peers anxiously at the intruder, and when disturbed expresses her alarm in no quiet terms. Fluttering from bush to bush she calls excitedly until, the danger removed, she can return once more to her duties.

The mistle thrush is one of our loudest, but most evocative, songsters.

The song thrush builds its nest in a great variety of situations. Early in the year it is usually set high up. A larch plantation or yew hedge or the ivy-covered bole of an elm are favourite sites: but later, with the growth of the year, the nests tend to come lower and hedge and bush provide ready cover. A few use even the ground, and some hide away in the thick rush growth in the hedge bottom.

A little farther up the lane a blackbird had its shapely nest in the low fork of a hedgerow elm. The cock's yellow bill and white-encircled eye attracted attention, and here again my tent was pitched. Nervous and never ready to accept the hide with that assurance which we so illogically expect from "garden" birds, both cock and hen tried my patience sorely. Yet the cock was assiduous in his duties and when his turn off the eggs came he was ever careful to bring food to his sitting mate. In between his foragings a high twig saw him challenge the world as possessor of his territory.

Several pairs of hedge sparrows nest in the lane. Little connected, despite its name, with our vulgar friend of the chimney-pots, the dunnock is comparatively secretive, and the number of birds actually seen in a single walk up the lane will give little indication of the number of nests which a diligent searcher can find. Yet its beautiful little nest and those eggs of brightest, unspotted blue are ample reward for success.

The finches are well represented in the lane. The topmost twigs of a thick hawthorn hold a bullfinch's nest, though only its characteristic flimsiness and the parent's anxious pipings reveal its identity, for its owners, despite their bright colours, are amongst the most retiring of birds.

Scattered here and there along the hedge greenfinches also have their nests, while from some slender twig the cock birds utter their drowsy notes the live-long summer day. The silvery note of the goldfinch, too, resounds along the lane in those favoured districts where the bird is common. Here, in Dorset, where are the lanes and hedgerows I know best, goldfinches are extraordinarily abundant, and their lovely little nests set high in the hedge are a common find.

Most abundant of the finches, the chaffinch is a familiar bird along the lane, and the brilliant colours of the cock immediately attract attention to him. The hen bird, too, for all her more subdued plumage is still an engaging bird, and as she flits anxiously from branch to branch with loud alarm note, her white wing patches render her conspicuous. At the nest both cock and hen share the duties of caring for the young, although the female would seem to bear the brunt of the incubation of the eggs.

In May, when the undergrowth thickens and the lazy beauty of the flowers is at its height, the hedgerow and lane become the province of the warblers. Here, where trailing bramble bushes separate the track from the higher hawthorn hedge and leave a few yards of rough scrub, whitethroats abound. From a tall spray the harsh alarm note of the cock, his crest raised, gives clear evidence of a secret deeply buried among the thick bushes. Careful search will reveal the cause of his anxiety. His flimsy nest is for all its untidy ends beautifully finished inside, and if seemingly too precarious to keep its nestling safe yet stands up to the strain remarkably well.

It is to be hoped that our remaining hedgerows, such valuable habitats for many species of animal and bird, can be saved from the wholesale destruction which has already accounted for so many miles of them. Few descriptions of small birds in their habitats better those of John Walpole-Bond in *A History of Sussex Birds* (1938). Here he picks out the lesser whitethroat, another bird which includes the traditional hedgerow among its favoured haunts.

As summer quarters the Lesser Whitethroat loves the uncouth clumps and thickets of lofty bushes (other than gorse) so prevalent in parts of downland and on certain of our "roughs" and commons, and it fairly revels in the tall, untrimmed hedgerow, particularly that aligning road and lane. It is often, too, an inmate of garden, shrubbery and pleasure-ground (even in big boroughs), to which, incidentally, all three, the common Whitethroat seldom condescends. It also likes very well those overgrown, jungle-like strips of cover decked here and there with fruit-trees, spots which from the ruins in their midst you know full well were once the holdings of cottages. Yet another fancied resort is the bush-clustered bank of pond and stream, and withy-beds, provided brambles and the like are present, sometimes prove attractive. Moreover, although the Lesser Whitethroat sedulously shuns woods and big plantations, where a shaw or small spinney of oak especially – this species delighting in devouring the larvae of the little green moth which so often devastates that tree – breaks the monotony of a hedge, often enough will a pair of these birds there be found, though the nest, of course, is either in a bush therein or else in the quickset so often adjacent.

We can recognise familiar birds both by their appearance and by their song. Len Howard described the fine song of the blackcap in *Birds As Individuals* (1952).

There is no music more lovely than the Blackcap's song. One day, in early June, a Blackcap was singing on the verge of a little wood where white-willows and ash trees blend their soft greens with the deeper shades of alder and oak. At first he flitted from tree to tree, his clear silvery notes, in short phrases, seeming flung to the air as lightly as the wind tossed the willow's long silvery leaves. Then he sang his full song, perched low on a branch with head upturned to the sunlit foliage, and it seemed the bird and the trees were inseparably linked in one great

21

harmonious inspiration. Together they expressed to perfection the music of colour and sound, for the windswept leaves in the sunlight were continually weaving fresh patterns of tone-colour that seemed a complete counterpart to the Blackcap's beautifully woven song. Phrases that began delicately were worked up to a finish on a gust of impetuous force, then a subdued, undulating song with notes flowing faster, until the finely turned fall of the cadence.

Close beside the wood was the Kingfisher's pool, where bright blue dragon-flies darted over the water like sparks struck from the Kingfisher. From the trees above the pool came the slower, deeper notes of a Blackbird. When Blackcap and Blackbird are heard together in full voice there seems no resemblance between their songs – the smaller bird naturally moulds his music on finer lines. But the quality of his song as a Warbler species corresponds with the Blackbird's as a Thrush species. Both are lovers of a tune on large lines. Blackcaps do much finely-woven warbling, but the greatest part of their song is when they break through this into a lovely, ringing tune. This may be sung without preliminary, but they often get a wonderful effect by working up their song, the big melody being held in reserve for the climax.

Song is not the only type of sound created by birds. Len Howard goes on to describe the antics of the goldfinches resident in her garden.

All round my cottage I have grown teazels for the Goldfinches. Sometimes twenty of these birds have been perched on them, extracting the seeds. In summer and autumn my garden is enlivened by a continuous trickle of their family chatter as the young flutter over flower-beds while the parents are gathering seeds of various plants, corn-flower and michaelmas daisies in their season being a favourite choice.

When extracting seeds from teazels they make a curious buzzing sound, suggesting a zither accompaniment to their musical twittering while they feed. A vibratory movement of the head when the beak is inserted into the seed-pocket seems necessary before the seeds can be pulled out, unless they are very ripe. This produces the buzzing, which carries a long distance, like the Woodpecker's drumming. I recently watched some young Goldfinches try unsuccessfully to extract seeds without the vibratory movement. Puzzled at their failure, they kept watching their parents' neat action but could not copy the vibratory trick and only moved their heads from side to side in the teazel pockets. This accomplished nothing, it made no sound, also failed to entice the

The long bill of the goldfinch enables it to tear into thistle-heads.

seed out, although they got their beaks well into the pockets. It was amusing to watch the puzzled expressions of the young birds, who kept turning to look at their parents then trying to imitate the actions. It reminded me of beginners at the violin who attempt to make vibrato, but the fingers will not vibrate. How the accomplished teazel performer made such a loud buzzing that carried so far at first puzzled me, but undoubtedly vibratory beak action on stiff surface has the effect of producing life and strength to the sound just as the violinist's tone gains life through use of vibrato, which intensifies vibrations and brings more natural harmonics into play.

My Goldfinches always nest high up in evergreen trees, where little can be seen of their nesting affairs. A friend once brought me a nestling

23

picked up in the road of a country town. It was only a few days old, still in down with half-open eyes, but black and gold was just beginning to show on its wings. The vitality of this immature bird was astonishing. When I put it into an improvised nest it scrambled out again and came towards me across the room to climb into the palm of my outstretched hand, there snuggling down to sleep. I fed it every hour during daylight on bread and milk, but the second day it shut its beak tight when I tried to give it this unnatural food, which disagreed with its digestion. No bird-seed of a suitable kind was then available. There were many Goldfinches in the garden and the nestling stretched up its head and cried at the sound of their voices, so I put the improvised nest on top of a hedge, leaving the nestling for an hour in the hope that some parent Goldfinch would hear its cries and, like Baldhead and his mate, adopt the orphan. When I returned the nestling had disappeared, nor was it to be found anywhere near the hedge.

Some birds are so difficult to observe that their calls are essential in recognising their presence at all. John Walpole-Bond described one such species, the hawfinch, in *A History of Sussex Birds* (1938).

It is advisable to master the gamut of the Hawfinch's vocal accomplishments, inasmuch as it is often solely by these that its presence in any area is indicated. For, as already shown, this is a creature of exemplary caution and coyness, and one, therefore, of which to get unbroken views is often desperately difficult. That is, except at the nest and, again, when with heavy, lilting flight it scurries at a fair height from one seclusion to another. Even does it dread motor-cars and bicycles, objects which long ere now most species have learnt to regard with the utmost disdain, often, be it added, in the case of the former, damnably to their detriment. Note, for instance, the deportment of this pair of Hawfinches first detected from afar by the conspicuous white frilling in wings and tail as they flash into a hedgerow bordering a shrubbery as you cycle slowly down the avenue aligning it. You are yet a good eighty yards distant when one bird hurries out of the hedge precipitately to be at once lost to view in the recesses of the background. Its fellow, leaving almost simultaneously, treats you little better. Merely does it take two short flights down the hedge away from you, making momentary use of a sapling as a half-way house, and it, too, has gone. Again, when after peas – and to procure such succulent fare Hawfinches will invade the most diminutive gardens into which at other times they hardly dare venture – it is only juveniles that are apt to relax vigilance. Talking of which reminds me that few gardeners realize that the damage done to the crops by repeated shooting of the pilferers far outweighs that engendered by the pilferers themselves, unless, of course, their numbers are excessive. Many other instances of this species' antipathy to surveillance could be afforded, but space forbids. Merely will I add that once only, away from the nest, has a Hawfinch allowed me, unambushed, a view at really close range. This bird was greedily breaking into hawthorn berries and apparently had eyes for nothing else. In any case, it permitted me to stand full in the open within a few feet of it for several minutes! Then suddenly it woke up. But instead of making tracks for the next parish, which is more or less what you would have expected, it simply sought a commissure in the trunk of a large beech close by. There so nicely did its plumage blend with the environment and so still did it stay, that even to me a witness of the act it was virtually invisible. This is not the only occasion on which I have seen a Hawfinch, when alarmed, carry out this clever deception.

Crossbills are also quiet feeders, as described in this further passage from Walpole-Bond.

Just ere surrendering one tree for another, and again when on the move, Crossbills constantly betray their whereabouts by loud characteristic cries. But when feeding they are inordinately tranquil. Then merely do they proclaim their presence by very gentle twitterings, by dropping to the ground discarded cones or by occasional whirring of wing as one branch is left for the next. Otherwise they steal and creep about like mice amidst the thickly foliaged tree-tops – these being vastly preferred to lowlier stances – where, unless light befriends you, even showy scarlet males are none too easy to see at will.

When just perching, a Crossbill is in some degree slightly cumbersome. For then its head, owing to a drastic drawing-out of the neck, looks decidedly top-heavy, whilst the stiff, upright pose of the body suggests a specimen abominably stuffed. But, mealing, the bird shows no lack of elegance. Its every action now is a sheer joy to behold, and provided you keep still, you shall sit, see and study to your heart's content at a range most intimate. Clinging to the branches in every conceivable posture, sometimes even back downwards, the acrobat sizes up the cones with the eyes of a connoisseur, and so soon as one amply supplied with seed is spied, dextrously is it detached from its short stem by means of the powerful bill which, curved and betwisted, makes a perfect instrument for the pruning. Then, grasping its booty with firm foot, it takes its fill of food, after which the now often worthless husk is let fall suddenly. In the case of large flocks feeding, many strobiles sometimes reach earth together, creating muffled volleys of sound, but at others there is merely heard a faint *feu-de-file* as one cone after the other rips and patters down through the maze of greenery to the carpet of "needles" beneath. And where a tree really rich in "fruit" has faithfully been harvested, round its base collects almost a small cart-load of "chaff." Sometimes a feeding flock for no ostensible reason takes sudden fright, whereupon nearly all its members scurry forth from their retreats a short way, but resume their seemingly self-interrupted feast almost immediately. At length they decide to go for good. Yet even so there generally stay behind a few gluttons, though these, too, depart before their fellows are well out of sight, the laggards flying their fastest to overtake them. And sometimes one of these stragglers in the middle of its meal when the signal sounds the retreat carries away the cone in its claws, loath to be deprived of even a particle.

The thrill of a starling roost is something which many have enjoyed, and Edmund Selous captures the atmosphere perfectly in *Bird Life Glimpses* (1905).

Starlings are most interesting when they flock, each night, to their accustomed roosting-place; in autumn, more especially, when their numbers are greatest. It is difficult to say, exactly, when the more commonplace instincts and emotions, which have animated the birds throughout the day, begin to pass into that strange excitement which heralds and pervades the home-flying. Comparatively early, however, in the afternoon many may be seen sitting in trees – especially orchard trees – and singing in a very full-throated manner. They are not eating the fruit; a dead and fruitless tree holds as many, in proportion to its size, as any of the other ones. Presently a compact flock comes down in an adjacent meadow, and the birds composing it are continually joined by many of the singing ones. Whilst watching them, other flocks begin to sweep by on hurrying pinions, and one notices that many of the high elm trees, into which they wheel, are already stocked with birds, whilst the air begins, gradually, to fill with a vague, babbling *susurrus*, that, blending with the stillness or with each accustomed sound, is perceived before it is heard – a felt atmosphere of song. One by one, or mingling with one another, these flocks leave the trees, and fly on towards the

Love them or hate them, starlings are great characters.

wood of their rest; but by that principle which impels some of any number, however great, to join any other great number, many detach themselves from the main stream of advance, and fly to the ever-increasing multitudes which still wheel, or walk, over the fields. It seems strange that these latter should, hitherto, have resisted that general movement which has robed each tree with life, and made a music of the air; but all at once, with a whirring hurricane of wings, they rise like brown spray of the earth, and, mounting above one of the highest elms, come sweeping suddenly down upon it, in the most violent and erratic manner, whizzing and zigzagging about from side to side, as they descend, and making a loud rushing sound with the wings, which, as with rooks, who do the same thing, is only heard on such occasions. They do not stay long, and as all the flocks keep moving onwards, the

27

immediate fields and trees are soon empty of birds. To follow their movements farther, one must proceed with all haste towards the roosting-place. About a mile's distance from it, at the tail of a little village, there is a certain meadow, emerald-green and dotted all over with unusually fine tall elms. In these, their accustomed last halting-place, the starlings, now in vast numbers, are swarming and gathering in a much more remarkable manner than has hitherto been the case. It is, always, on the top of the tree that they settle, and, the instant they do so, it becomes suddenly brown, whilst there bursts from it, as though from some great natural musical box, a mighty volume of sound that is like the plash of waters mingled with a sharper, steelier note – the dropping of innumerable needles on a marble floor. On a sudden the sing-song ceases, and there is a great roar of wings, as the entire host swarm out from the tree, make a wheel or half-wheel or two, close about it, and then, as though unable to go farther, seem drawn back into it again, by some strong, attractive force. Or they will fly from one tree to another of a group, swarming into each, and presenting, as they cluster in myriads about it, before settling, more the appearance of a vast swarm of bees, or some other insects, than of birds. These flights out from the trees, always very sudden, seem, sometimes, to be absolutely instantaneous; whilst in every case it is obvious that vast numbers must move in the same twinkle of time, as though they were threaded together.

All this time, fresh bands are continuing to arrive, draining different areas of the country. From tree to field, from earth to sky, again, is flung and whirled about the brown, throbbing mantle of life and joy; nature grows glad with sound and commotion; children shout and clap their hands; old village women run to the doors of cottages to gaze and wonder – the starlings make them young. Blessed, harmless community! The men are out, no guns are there, it is like the golden age. And now it is the final flight, or, rather, the final many flights, for it is seldom – perhaps never – that all, or even nearly all, arrive together at the roosting-place. As to other great things, so to this daily miracle there are small beginnings; the wonder of it grows and grows. First a few quite small bands are seen flying rapidly, yet soberly, which, as they near or pass over the silent wood – their pleasant dormitory – sweep outwards, and fly restlessly round in circles – now vast, now narrow – but of which it is ever the centre. "Then comes wandering by" one single bird – apart, cut off, by lakes of lonely air, from all its myriad companions. Some three or four follow separately, but not widely sundered; then a dozen together, which the three or four join;

then another small band, which is joined by one of those that have gone before it, itself now, probably, swollen by amalgamation. Now comes a far larger band, and this one, instead of joining, or being joined by, any other, divides, and, streaming out in two directions, follows one or other of those circling streams of restless, hurrying flight, that girdles, as with a zone of love and longing, the darksome, lonely-lying wood. A larger one, still, follows; and now, more and faster than the eye can take it in, band grows upon band, the air is heavy with the ceaseless sweep of pinions, till, glinting and gleaming, their weary wayfaring turned to swiftest arrows of triumphant flight – toil become ecstasy, prose an epic song – with rush and roar of wings, with a mighty commotion, all sweep, together, into one enormous cloud. And still they circle; now dense like a polished roof, now disseminated like the meshes of some vast all-heaven-sweeping net, now darkening, now flashing out a million rays of light, wheeling, rending, tearing, darting, crossing, and piercing one another – a madness in the sky. All is the starlings' now; they are no more birds, but a part of elemental nature, a thing affecting and controlling other things. Through them one sees the sunset; the sky must peep through their chinks. Surely all must now be come. But as the thought arises, a black portentous cloud shapes itself on the distant horizon; swiftly it comes up, gathering into its vast ocean the small streams and driblets of flight; it approaches the mighty host and is the mightier – devours, absorbs it – and, sailing grandly on, the vast accumulated multitude seems now to make the very air, and be, itself, the sky.

As a rule, this great concourse separates, again, into two main, and various smaller bodies, and it is now, and more especially amongst the latter, that one may witness those beautiful and varied evolutions which are, equally, a charm to the eye and a puzzle to the mind. Each band, as it circles rapidly round, permeated with a fire of excitement and glad alacrity, assumes diverse shapes, becoming, with the quickness of light, a balloon, an oil-flask, a long, narrow, myriad-winged serpent, rapidly thridding the air, a comet with tail streaked suddenly out, or a huge scarf, flung about the sky in folds and shimmers. A mass of flying birds must, indeed, assume some shape, though it is only on these occasions that one sees such shapes as these. More evidential, not only of simultaneous, but, also of similar motion throughout a vast body, are those striking colour changes that are often witnessed. For instance, a great flock of flying birds will be, collectively, of the usual dark-brown shade. In one instant – as quickly as Sirius twinkles from green to red, or red to gold – it has become a light grey. Another instant, and it is, again, brown, and this whilst the rapidly-moving host seems to occupy the same space in the air, so lightning-quick have been the two flashes of colour and motion – for both may be visible – through the living medium; as though one had said, "One, two," or blinked the eyes twice. Yet in the sky all is a constant quantity; the sinking sun has neither rushed in nor out, on all the wide landscape round no change of light and shade has fallen, and other bands of moving birds maintain their uniform hue. Obviously the effect has been due to a sudden change of angle in each bird's body, in regard to the light – as when one rustles a shot-silk dress – and this change has shot, in the same second of time, through myriads of bodies. Sometimes the light of the sky will show, suddenly, like so many windows, through a multitude of spaces, which seem to be at a set and regular distance from one another; and then, again, be as suddenly not seen, the whole mass becoming opaque to the eye, as before. Here, again, the effect, which is beautiful, can only be produced by a certain number of the birds just giving their wings a slant, or otherwise shifting their posture in the air, all at the same instant of time. This, at least, is the only way in which I can explain it.

Birds on the wing in large numbers can provide breathtaking and emotional sights such as this. Some birds can truly be called "masters of the air" in both speed and agility, and these include the swift, here described by John Walpole-Bond in *A History of Sussex Birds* (1938).

The Swift's life is mainly of the air. No bird is more tireless, none for its size so vigorous or muscular, few the species that excel it in speed. Towards evening, especially, the birds become very boisterous, particularly at their nesting-haunts. There, round and round the actual breeding-sites, in small detachments they dash madly, first with ultra-rapid quiverings of their scimitar wings, which now look like strained wires vibrating, then with clean, cutting glides, pinions held rigidly erect and often almost touching above their backs. At intervals they scream, now lustily, now demurely. On a sudden two birds branch off from the main body. They start by flying with greater celerity than ever, fairly plunging along in right giddy fashion. But the next second finds them by comparison more sedate. By and by return is made to the main gathering, where their identity is straightway lost in the fast-whirling throng of dusky, anchor-shaped imp-birds still revelling in their frantic game of follow-my-leader. Later in the evening, leaving their low or comparatively low elevation, they mount into the

The swift's shape is a guide to its way of life – fast and aerial.

firmament intent on their customary nightly "fling." At first, perhaps – indeed, generally (unless, of course, you have traced their career from the beginning) – it is their now subdued screams, mere shadows of sound, descending through the still, warm fragrance of this growing summer night that bid you look up. Then, if you are Argus-eyed, you shall discern through the gathering gloom of twilight many black specks dimly printed on the waning azure of a spent sky. These specks are, of course, Swifts. At the distance and owing as well to the hazy half-light they hardly appear to be travelling at all or at best only very slowly. Yet in reality they are travelling very fast indeed, though possibly not quite up to maximum form. Presently they rise to such a height that even powerful glasses fail to hold them. Some of the merry-makers rush roostwards about 10 p.m. (true time), but all are not home till well after midnight. To this I can testify from long and repeated nocturnal vigils in the Horsham belfry.

Flying skills are nevertheless not confined to the more spectacular species. The Canon Charles E. Raven (*Bird Haunts and Bird Behaviour*, 1929) described pied wagtails.

The Pied Wagtail is so much more a bird of lawns and duckponds that one cannot properly assign him to the stream. Yet his flickerings from stone to stone, his agility in the air as he twists in and out to secure a gnat, his buoyant and irrepressible energy add a charm that we should sadly miss. He is like an urchin at the seaside, bubbling over with merriment and high spirits, with jaunty airs of comic dignity setting off his lapses into gleeful acrobatics. Now he poses solemnly on a rock, jerking his tail and full of self-satisfaction: now he throws himself into rapturous pursuit of an invisible insect: now he flings catherine-wheels as his quarry dodges his onset: now he returns, the successful hunter, to swallow his prey, and start out afresh.

He found the grey wagtail to be more of a bird of the stream.

The Grey Wagtail is far more truly a bird of the beck. I knew him first as a migrant calling for a few hours at Cambridge on his way to the south in March or October and outshining the daffodils or the falling elm leaves with the brilliancy of his breast. Of all our birds he is by common consent the most elegant alike in form and colour: indeed, though very many are more gorgeously apparelled, there is not in the world any to rival him for grace of outline and perfection of design. His yellow is the pure hue that is the despair of artists, free from all suspicion of green or brown, a clear saffron ranging from the poignancy of dawn to the full blaze of sunset, a tint that no pigments and hardly any flowers can match. His grey back and the black cravat beneath his

The grey wagtail is one of the most attractive birds in Britain.

chin, themselves of an almost sombre neatness, are incomparably fitted to redeem his splendour from garishness and to create an air of distinction. His long black tail with its edging of white emphasises the slender lines of his build, and gives a dainty finish to a perfect design. Here on the beck he arrives with early April, starts at once to explore, and in a few weeks settles down to married life and the upbringing of a family. In August you can see the brood, still together, flashing like brimstone butterflies over grey rocks and umber water, travelling up the rivulets as I have seen them beneath Glydir Fach or joining the Rock Pipits on the seaweed of the shore as they do at Ringabella.

Not so familiar, but embodying the true essence of the brook, is the dipper, with its remarkable swimming and diving skills. Canon Raven describes its behaviour in *Bird Haunts and Bird Behaviour* (1929).

The Dipper is the real spirit of the beck, the incarnation of its moods, the genius of running water. He is there all the year round, there and nowhere else. You may see the other species anywhere; they would survive if the mountains and all their streams were carried into the midst of the sea: the Dipper would perish with them. He is supremely specialised: structure, character and habits are exactly adapted to a particular way of life in a particular environment. Alone among the passerines he has given up the land for the water, and achieved the skill of the fisherman with limbs appropriate to woodcraft.

My first acquaintance with him was made when I had just learned (slowly and with peril) to ride a bicycle, and set up a record by pushing myself from Chester to Llangollen. Valle Crucis was the goal of the journey, but my memory of the ruined abbey is less vivid than of the little brown and white birds on the river at Berwyn. Here was something new and unexpected, a little creature like a stumpy-tailed Blackbird or an overgrown Wren plunging recklessly into boiling eddies, scuttering through currents that must surely sweep it to destruction, and yet emerging unscathed and without flurry or sense of escape.

Since then I have seen him often and in many places – indeed, whenever kind chance has led me to the hills. His activity kept me fascinated for a long August afternoon on the Lledr at Pontypant. In June we spent a happy hour watching a pair that had evidently got a young brood on a brook under the northern slopes of the Lammermuirs, when the hen surprised us by perching on a tree and running up the

The life of the dipper is tied to its watery environment.

branches like a Nuthatch. But he has never been an intimate of mine, and always his behaviour strikes me afresh as unexpected and freakish. I do not know him well enough to associate his habits with his shape, and am always expecting him to leave the water and join the thrushes in the hedgerows.

He cannot keep out of the water for many minutes, and in it reveals a technique unlike that of any other bird. Here on the beck he has his favourite places for bathing and fishing, places where the water is shallow rushing down in wavelets over a bottom scoured of mud, and the stones lie close to the surface and here and there break above it. A tree stands by the brink and its roots are restful and concealing. Sit still and watch the Dipper at his work. He has preened himself and sung, and is now ready for a meal.

He sets off downstream along the brink, turning over dry leaves and grass, peering into crannies, searching the flotsam washed up in the inlets, running out into the water where the bank is steep, and swimming for a few yards where the current slides smoothly by the shore. Swimming he sits low and rather flat, holding his head well forward and close to the surface. In this position the white on his chest blends with the ripple in front of him, and he looks much more like a water-rat than a bird. His colour is, of course, excellent camouflage in broken water, and his jerky actions, pauses and sudden jumps, are always rat-like.

Reaching the downward limit of his fishing ground he starts to work upstream, and leaves the bank for the mid-current. Now is the time to study his methods under water; for though some of his prey is caught as it floats much of it is obtained from the bottom where the caddis-larvae trail their houses of stalks and gravel over the pebbles. His pursuit of them depends upon the depth to be searched. In the shallows he darts into the flood, bobbing in and out, but holding fast to the ground. He moves very swiftly in a spasm of energy as restless as the stream. In deeper places he dives, springing into the water head first and using his wings to carry on the impetus of his plunge. When fishing he usually dives right into the current; while his head is lowered, the pressure of the water inevitably sinks him. But his submergence is short, lasting only a very few seconds and covering barely a foot, till his momentum is exhausted, and he flings up his head, rises to the surface and lets the stream carry him back to his starting-point.

In this chapter we have merely dipped into the literature concerning some of our common and familiar birds, but I hope that the extracts quoted will inspire you to look on them with a new and appreciative eye. After all, it is the common birds that we see most of and we should ensure that they remain common and familiar. Some of them so easily slip away as their habitat is eroded or disturbed, almost unnoticed until, perhaps, it is too late.

2 SEABIRDS AND ISLANDS

Seabirds, and the places they inhabit – the oceans themselves, offshore stacks, rocks and rugged, rock-bound islands, cliffs, beaches of sand or shingle, dunes or islands smothered with sweet-smelling red campion, bluebells or sea pink – these romantic birds and places evoke very special feelings, a yearning to be out with them, smelling the sea, feeling the wind. James Fisher (one of the great seabird and sea coast enthusiasts) and Ronald Lockley summed up the fascination especially well in *Seabirds* (1954).

The heroes of our story are rather over a hundred species of birds whose life is a sea-life, whose habits enable them to earn at least part of their living in, or on, salt water, and which have been seen in the Atlantic Ocean north of the Equator.

The North Atlantic is the scene of our book, the great ocean that is now the most travelled by man. Its two sides are provided with an almost equal variety of sea-birds: sixty-eight species, or rather over half are common to both. Of all Atlantic countries Britain, considering its size, has the greatest number of sea-bird species; with no less than eighty, it can boast on its list all but six of those that have been seen on the Atlantic coast of Europe. The British Isles therefore make a good headquarters for a survey of the sea-birds of the North Atlantic. In Britain, and from Britain, the writers of this book have explored the eastern Atlantic sea-bird stations, and enjoyed many fine islands and memorable experiences. One or the other of us has sought the sea-birds south to the frigate-petrel burrows of the Salvages, near the Canary

Islands; north to the ivory-gull colonies on the nunataks that rise from the ice-cap of Spitsbergen; or from 30°N nearly to 80°N, a distance of more than three thousand miles; west we have ranged to Iceland, the Faeroes, Rockall, St. Kilda and the Blaskets of the Kerry coast; east we have travelled to Heligoland, and as far as Laesö in the Kattegat and Gotland in the Baltic, with their off-lying islands of sea-birds. There is no coastal county in England, Wales and Scotland that has not been visited by us both, and not one in Ireland that has not been visited by one of us.

No good British sea-bird cliff or island has been overlooked in our search for what the naturalist searches for; our experience and enjoyment has been long and continuous because both of us are, each in his somewhat different way, obsessed with sea-birds and with islands. We have spent a combined total of nearly seventy years sea-bird watching.

Such obsession was not confined to Fisher and Lockley. In his book *A Fauna of the Outer Hebrides* (1888), co-written with T. E. Buckley, J. A. Harvie-Brown describes his impressions during a visit to North Rona, one of the most remote islands in Britain.

About 3 p.m. of June 18th, 1887, we landed for the second time on North Ronay with perfect ease, even easier than in 1885. Meanwhile the yacht stood off and on in the East Bay, opposite the landing-place known as Geodha-Stoth. On this occasion, being anxious to complete my previous survey of 1885, which was a very hurried and unsatisfactory one, I turned my back upon the Fork-tailed Petrels' end of the island, and struck away across the rich carpet of sea-pink and short sweet grass of the lower northern peninsula. The sea-pink, which grows in continuous profusion over the whole surface, filled the air with delicious fragrance, faint but sweet. The rich but short pasturage is strewn with scattered boulders, and in places these have been piled together, no doubt by many previous generations of shepherds and crofters, and formed into many rough sheepfolds and shelters. Oyster-catchers were abundant and aggressive; perhaps nowhere have I seen them so numerous and tame. Gulls were constant in their cries and attendance upon us, the species being Greater and Lesser Black-backed Gulls and Herring-gulls. Eider-ducks were constantly crossing my path, lumbering along in heavy flight, or squattering off their nests, or swimming in sheltered creeks along with their newly-hatched young. Puffins were bobbing about, or ducking head first into the crevices of the cairns, every loose heap of boulders holding some proportion of the general colony. Hundreds of these birds, disturbed by Dr Heddle from favourite resting-places alongshore, streamed continuously past. Shags innumerable lined the lower talus of débris close to the rocky coast, or sat fanning their wings on the rocks themselves. These ranges of loose stones are arranged in two distinct tiers, one along the higher or westward cliff-tops of the peninsula, the other just above the solid rocky shore of the eastern slope. The Shags were the inhabitants of the gloomy caves of the more lofty southern portion of Ronay, which penetrate the northern faces of the East and West Horns. Rock Pipits were not so abundant as observed elsewhere, though there appeared to be no lack of suitable nesting-ground. Crossing to the west side of the peninsula, I walked over a great stretch of unbroken and continuous bare gneiss, which held in its hollows wind-caught spray-pools, covered with green sea-weeds carried up from the shore. On one of these pools of considerable size, which occupied a hollow close within a ledge of rock, not more than five feet from the cliff-edge, an Eider-duck and her young were swimming about, and Black Guillemots seemed to use it as an occasional playground. On this side, huge caverns, göes, groups, and

The cormorant is, on a European scale, a scarce and local bird.

rock-arches, stacks, and detached masses of rock, abound, and at once attract attention; and the booming of unbroken Atlantic waves, and giant rollers lashing deep into their recesses, and filling often to the roof some of the great arches, proved a very fascinating scene to me. Here the actual element of water was seldom visible, save glistening with a wondrous green lustre through the white foam of the retreating surges. A dunlin or two sprang from the sides of the rocky, spray-holding hollows, and a flock of Turnstones circled round the island out of sight. The highest portion of the cliff here is not more than 60 feet, but the extreme wildness of the scene rather gained than lost by the lesser altitude, and the strength of ocean's waves seemed almost to crush their insignificance. On a flat-topped summit of the cliff was a large resting colony of puffindom, which evidently had its nesting holes amongst the great tier of disintegrating gneiss, which ran parallel with the cliff-top, but at a slightly higher elevation, about 50 yards further inland, and which ridge forms the summit of the seapink-covered slope, of which we have already made mention.

After some biscuits and potted meat, and a pull at Silver's water-bottle, Heddle and I climbed the eastern top of Ronay, 355 feet, but mist obscured the view. We then crossed over the green valley and slope facing the south, and so along the second hillside to the ruins of the old village, the church mentioned by Muir, the underground houses, the crofting lands of the former inhabitants, and the breeding-place of the Fork-tailed Petrels. In the ruined masonry of the old church we heard the churring of the Fork-tailed Petrels, probably "churching their wooing," but a desecrating blow from the doctor's hammer upon some garnet-holding lump of rock silenced their revelry, and they stopped, much as a clock would do when "run down," and I was left lamenting.

Coming round the high cliffs to the west – or on the Western Horn, – the Peregrine soon asserted himself, his fine wild challenge being the first notice of his presence. The cliffs of this portion are very fine indeed, and have a peculiar grandeur, partly owing to a gigantic gable-end of MacCulloch's red granite seam, which, stretching across the whole southern portion of Ronay in a vast dyke some 20 feet thick, and interrupting the darker coloured masses of hornblende, stands out of the cliff with a noble curve, giving rich colour to the precipice, and frowning defiant o'er the deep. This is best seen from a point to westward, but a very fine general view of these cliffs facing the north-west can also be had from a spur of the north peninsula, close to a vast cave which runs almost through the rock or neck of this peninsula, and is joined about half-way across by a deep creux, or "swallow," which descends to the sea-cave at an angle of about 65°. The following day – being the 19th June – we landed again, principally to allow of photographs being taken, and Mr Norrie was successful in obtaining several fine views. Among the old ruins, C., – our steward and cook on board – and I dug away for an hour. The Fork-tailed Petrels' eggs were much harder to reach than on the occasion of our former visit in 1885, being in much more secure retreats, and deeper in the masonry. We took six eggs, and I kept three birds.

On the face of the N. W. precipice or Horn of Ronay, where there is a considerable broken surface suitable for such birds nesting, I saw six or eight Fulmar Petrels skimming, as is their wont, close to and fro past the cliff-face and top. I saw one alight twice at the same place, about 50 yards west of the granite cliff before mentioned. On returning to this place in the afternoon, but from a further off vantage spot near a large Kittiwake colony in a cave, I could not see the Fulmars, though at once, on going to the west of the granite cliff, I saw them again, and several flew very close past where I was sitting, just as I have seen them do also on St Kilda; but they rarely flew *over the land*, almost always over the sea. It seemed quite evident that this part of the cliff is the only bit frequented by these birds. I did see *one* Fulmar fly with tremendous speed from west to east across the neck of the peninsula, as if he did not feel himself at home over the land; I never saw one fly at such speed over the sea. After making some of the above notes I crept on hands and knees to the edge, and craned over to get a better view of the face; and my delight was great when I saw one Fulmar sitting, apparently on its nest. Whether there were any more or not, I cannot say, as buttresses of hornblende and granite intervened and obstructed my view. Wishing to see if she were breeding, I threw down several small stones, and, not without some trouble, managed at last to dislodge her. My disappointment was as great as my previous delight, when I saw an empty nest. But the grassy nose on which it was placed showed a perfectly formed cup or wide depression about the size of a soup-plate, scraped or dusted out of a flat piece of seapink turf, and apparently ready for the reception of an egg. I looked around for a long, long time, trying to catch sight of a herring-gull, lest possibly this might have been its nest; but no, not one was visible. Whether it really is a nest of the Fulmar, or merely a resting-place, must, however, still remain undecided.

Harvie-Brown's enthusiasm for North Rona was shared by Frank Fraser Darling, when he visited the same island many years later. He describes the experience in *Island Years* (1940).

We were in the east bay of Rona and my spirit rose above seasickness, for it is the wonder of that first view that has remained. My heart was full of sheer joy. But immediately the great practical question leapt into my mind – should we be able to land on this island which is notoriously bad for landing? For the moment that was not my business, and wonder returned as I looked at the hundreds of thousands of sea birds which flew from the cliffs, startled by this most unusual advent of humanity and a ship.

It was tremendous and awe-inspiring. The swarms of puffins, guillemots and razorbills circled like bees from the hive of the cliff; kittiwakes flashed white from every coign of the rock face which would hold a nest, and fulmar petrels glided silently on motionless wings like small monoplanes. Shags flew hither and thither, black and cumbrous compared with the grace of the smaller birds. The sound of it all was the most thrilling a bird watcher knows – the composite skirl of a million throats proclaiming that it is summer. All I could think in that moment of wonder was – and we are going to live here and know every bit of this place as if it were home. After all, it was home.

The thrill of the ceaseless activity of a seabird colony has made a great impression on many writers. In his book *The Atlantic Islands* (1948), Kenneth Williamson tells of his visit to more northerly islands, the Faeroes.

When our boat had pitched and tossed its way through the racing tide between the islands we gained the shelter of Mykines' southern coast, and sailed more peacefully in the shadow of the mighty cliffs. The land rises in alternating terraces of naked basalt bands and steep grassy shelves reaching up to the overhanging pall of cold, grey mists shrouding the island's summit. Great daubs of green ground spill out of the land, slopping over the cliff-face to the sea, and here and there immense grassy buttresses, stippled with the white fronts of innumerable puffins sunning themselves outside the earthy portals of their homes, bolster the fortress wall. Everywhere against this wall, and covering the dappled expanse of the waves and the mottled sky, are countless thousands of birds: without the actual experience, one would find it hard to believe that any place on earth could be so lavishly stocked. We seemed to sail through a world seething with the eager, throbbing life of a tremendous hive, thrumming with a million wing-beats and gay everywhere with movement and bright colour.

For a time the birds around us were almost exclusively puffins and fulmars. The puffins hurried to one side, paddling furiously or taking headlong dives to get out of our way; but the fulmars seemed inquisitively interested in the boat and time after time swept low across the bows, or sidled up on the wind to look at us out of their cold, expressionless eyes. Gull-like in the distance with their white bodies and greyish wings, they are curiously changed when close at hand; their bodies are short and fat, their yellow bills a different shape because they are among the few birds to possess a nose – a short horny tube along the top of the beak – and their wings straight-cut and rigid as they swing round on the wind, not sharply angled like those of a gull.

As we drew farther to the west it became obvious that two species were largely responsible for the character of the scene, and that although others were present they were noticeable only by the sudden contrast they made with the two hordes, the puffins and kittiwakes, which shared between them the onshore and offshore realms. The puffins flew past in busy crowds, trailing little streaks of bright colour where their legs and splayed feet supplemented inadequate tails. All around the boat the water was darkly mottled with the birds, and the air vibrated to the thrum of their fast-winnowing wings. Not a second passed by without a spattering of orange-vermilion paddles as birds leapt out of our path, to rise clear or change their minds and vanish as suddenly as they had appeared in a headlong plunge under the waves.

The disturbance of land, sea and air was chaotic. The puffins were the nature and the spirit of the scene everywhere except in the immediate vicinity of the cliffs, where the kittiwakes floated as thickly against the dark backdrop as snowflakes against a midwinter sky, stealing the picture from them. Their voices rose in a perpetual threnody of sound, and although the sheer walls were plastered white with sitting birds, it seemed that thousands more swirled madly on restless wings. By contrast of colour, voice or form other species intruded on the scene. Their lithe fork-tailed bodies and shrill screams announced the arctic terns. The crimson legs and dazzling white blur of the black guillemots' wing-patches attracted attention to this most lovable of all sea-birds. Occasionally the slender brown silhouettes of arctic skuas caught the eye as they planed past above, looking for some laden kittiwake to rob. Herring and lesser blackback gulls flew past, looking lonely indeed among the crowds of auks and kittiwakes. Once I caught sight of a single gannet some way out at sea: otherwise the only evidence that a gannetry existed close at hand was provided by the gleaming white caps of Flatidrangur and Pikarsdrangur, twin stacks at the south-western corner of the holm, on which were sitting innumerable birds.

At length we turned into the landing-place, a large rock-lined cleft open to the south-west, and obviously the kind of place where disembarkation is always a little uncertain unless the wind and tide and sea are just right. One could well imagine the inaccessibility of this small cove under certain complications of these elements, so all-important in the lives of small maritime communities; and it was significant that the boathouses were perched at the end of a promontory a good fifty or sixty feet above the sea, out of harm's way of the winter storms. I had been told during the journey that it is usual for Mykines to be isolated for long periods in the winter months, and that sometimes the Christmas mail does not reach the inhabitants until March! It was not at all difficult to visualise this place with the white surf seething at the rocky walls, nor did one need much experience of small islands to guess what terrors a heavy ground swell would have within this narrow *gjógv*.

To-day conditions were peaceful enough, and without difficulty we jumped ashore and made our way across the sloping rocks to the foot of the steep pathway which is in reality the beginning of the village street. Very soon I saw the village and its spacious green *bour* for the first time, for during the approach by boat one sees only the jumble of *hjallar* and boathouses on the point. The village lies low in the valley, pleasing and picturesque like all Faeroe *bygdir*, because each house is different in size, shape, and hue from its neighbours. Some are brightly coloured, or painted white, and in contrast there are the older houses with their sod roofs and pitch-black walls. Clustering about them all are dingy outhouses of stone, or stone and wood combined, and the meat-drying *hjallar* of upright wooden planks set an inch or so apart, so that flickering shafts of daylight seem to ripple through the hut as you stroll by. Below the houses runs the little stream, crossed by a concrete bridge, and standing on a knoll above the northern half of the settlement is the white church of simple, traditional design, and near to it another white building with a red roof that is self-evidently the school. Below this cultural seat I found the house of Abraham Abrahamsen, with whom I was to stay.

Here on the ocean fringe is a place that is at once one of the most wholesome and characteristic of Faeroe settlements, quite unspoilt by the influence of modern civilisation which has permeated the fishing towns on other islands. And it is, moreover, more worthy than any place I have visited to be called a birdman's paradise. Not only are the birds here in prodigal abundance, living amid the loveliest surroundings you will find in this strange and beautiful group of islands; but they are also, as perhaps nowhere else in the world, so closely bound up with the daily life of the people and the economic structure of their community that it is quite impossible to study them without considering their relationship to mankind. Mykines, as a result of centuries of winter hardships and isolation, has learned to live alone. The chief concern of the fruitful summer must always be the provision of sufficient food to tide the people over the harsh and unproductive winter months. The bird-fowling, by which the chief of the island's natural resources is conserved, keeps this village alive, and at the same time helps to maintain in this pleasant place those customs and traditions which have made Faeroe folk-culture unique in the civilised world.

Each birdwatcher dedicated to seabirds has favourite sites at which to observe them. In *In Search of Northern Birds* (1941), Seton Gordon was especially impressed with Hermaness, Shetland.

Gannets dominate the scene around Stac-an-armin, St Kilda.

To bird lovers, Hermaness is of special interest since as I have earlier mentioned, the great skua nests on the promontory. In 1861 Saxby found only five or six pairs of great skuas here, and believed that the extermination of the race was near. Richard Kearton in one of his books mentions that when he visited Hermaness about the year 1897 there were thirteen pairs: when my friend and I saw the colony in 1937 it consisted of no less than ninety pairs. That the great skua was not exterminated on Hermaness is due to the family of Edmondston of Buness, who owned the land. They built a hut in view of the nesting birds and appointed a man to keep watch on the colony and prevent egg collectors and 'men with guns' visiting it. The pioneer work of this well-known Unst family has since been carried on by the Royal Society for the Protection of Birds.

It was a July morning when my friend and I climbed to Hermaness, and high in the clear sky white clouds drifted from the western ocean. During the whole of the two miles' walk from Burra Firth to Hermaness the climber is in skua country. The lower slopes are tenanted mainly by Arctic skuas, graceful long-winged birds of which there were more than a hundred pairs present that summer. In July, when the young are hatched and are hiding in the heather, the parent skuas on the approach of their enemy, man, stand in prominent positions with open beaks, fluttering their wings as though injured. This trick is played in the hopes of distracting attention from the defenceless young. We walked past successive pairs of acting Arctic skuas until we reached, near a small tarn, the great skua colony and were attacked fiercely by one after another of these large brown-plumaged birds which at times call to mind the buzzard in their easy flight and graceful soaring. But the buzzard's wing primaries when soaring are sometimes open: those of the great skua are always tightly closed. It is hard to avoid ducking one's head at the swoop of a great skua: the bird with a rush of wings approaches gracefully but apparently relentlessly at the height of one's head and at the speed of an express train. When seen together – and the Arctic skua fiercely pursues any great skua which may fly over its territory – the swift, dashing flight of the Arctic skua and the heavier flight of the great skua are interesting to compare.

As we watched the skuas on the most northerly cape of Britain a cloud approached from the Atlantic and Hermaness for a brief space was shrouded in thin mist; but when the cloud passed the day became even clearer than before. Surrounding us was an immense sea horizon. Only to the south was land visible, and here the Shetland Isles lay beneath the summer sun. Beyond the island of Yell was what is called the mainland of Shetland: the isle of Bressay, near Lerwick and almost 50 miles distant, was plainly seen. Beneath us were Muckle Flugga and the neighbouring Vesta Skerry, snow-white in the sun. This whiteness was from the great gannet colony which nest here. The birds are comparatively recent comers, for they first arrived here in 1920, and each year since then have increased.

We descended the seaward grassy slopes of Hermaness, with Bruce the bird-watcher as our guide, and found ourselves at the edge of a formidable cliff, down which led a narrow sheep track. Considerable care was necessary to descend this track, and we crept warily from ledge to ledge, with the waves sparkling in the sun far beneath us, rows and groups of puffins standing beside their burrows eyed us with curiosity. Fulmars sailed past so near that they almost touched us and on the rocks below grey Atlantic seals slept. The climber when he has descended with relief to the cliff foot finds himself in a country as grand and majestic as any to be found in Britain. Not even in the Hebrides, or on St. Kilda, have I found cliff scenery to equal that of Hermaness.

Spectacular scenery may play a large part in creating feelings of awe and wonder. The birds alone, however, can induce such a mood. Seton Gordon describes some of the seabirds of Hoy, Orkney, in the same book (see p. 44).

It was a grey morning when I passed the old manse that stands beside the shore amid sheltering trees. Above the manse there were curlews on the moors where the yellow saxifrage, *Saxifraga azoides*, grew beside the road. Above the township of Breibusta pale blue peat smoke rose from old houses and beyond Breibusta were the great cliffs of Hoy. But these cliffs were entirely hidden from my sight, for the ocean mist, gently rising and falling on light aerial currents, bathed them to their feet. Fulmars glided silently along the edge of the cliffs (I noticed that these birds did not, as on Unst, venture over the land) and kittiwakes and guillemots stood on their nesting ledges. As we climbed towards the high cliffs my friend and I entered the cloud at a height of 500 feet above the sea, then for more than six hours followed the margin of this great sea precipice, moving through a country of dense, clammy vapours with puffins as our guides. So long as we were in sight of these quaint birds we knew that we were at the edge of the precipice, for the mist was so close that we could see no more than a few yards. Strange shapes which might have been fortresses or great castles appeared before us, then were lost in the fog. Sometimes the mist thinned and the puffins could be seen more clearly, and when we had almost reached St. John's Head, where the cliff drops a sheer 1140 feet to the sea, the air for a few brief moments cleared and we could see, through a rift in the cloud, the inky blue waters of the Atlantic far beneath us. We were then perhaps thirty feet from a waterfall which fell over the precipice. Beside this white stream puffins stood near their burrows, and it was curious to see them perched in the spray of a hill waterfall more than 1000 feet above the sea, with heather in blossom beside them. Surely this mountain nesting site was a great contrast to the puffins' seafaring life during nine of the twelve months of the year.

Very slowly, with majestic grandeur, the cloud rolled away from the top of the cliff, which then showed dark like an island in an aerial sea. A family of ravens took advantage of this brief clear interval to fly westwards along the cliff, moving leisurely through the calm air. Thousands of puffins flew, elf-like, backwards and forwards above and across the cliff: very dark they seemed against the white sea mist below them. Some of the puffins were flying several hundred feet above us, and must have been at least 1500 feet above the ocean's surface. An immense number of puffins nest on the sea precipices of Hoy. In the following summer, on the outward passage to Iceland, I watched, hour after hour, puffins flighting in from their fishing grounds towards Hoy. The birds were converging on that island from all quarters, and thousands must have passed our vessel even when Hoy was scarcely visible astern.

Having drunk in the atmosphere of the pulsating seabird cities, we can now turn to specific groups of seabirds. Fisher and Lockley in *Seabirds* (1954) observed petrels in detail.

Of all the birds which frequent the North Atlantic Ocean, the petrels or, as they are known today to ornithologists, the tube-noses, appear to be the most perfectly adapted to its frequent wild moods and heavy storms. A chapter on their life-histories would be incomplete, therefore, without a full discussion on the pelagic phases – little understood until recently – of the petrel's year. Only those who have seen from a ship at sea the fragile-looking storm-petrel or the long-winged shearwater or the more gull-like fulmar ride out a whole winter gale can realise, and admire and respect fully, this perfection of adaptation to the extreme conditions of environment. The more savage the gale, in fact, the more easily do these graceful birds seem to ride upon the salty air, and skim the heaving surface of the sea with more perfect mastery. Sustained by the winds, they are able to glide nearer to ships, and the human observer is able to study them. But formerly the superstitious mariner regarded the appearance of the small petrels close to the ship as an ill omen, accompanied as they were by storms.

The perfection of oceanic flight is seen best among the largest petrels, the true albatrosses, which, in the Atlantic, are confined principally to the southern hemisphere and rarely wander north of the equator. The structure of the very long slender wing of the albatross, with its long humeral bones and strong rigid primaries, makes normal wing-beating, such as that of the storm-petrel, difficult, and progression is almost entirely by gliding. The flight of the shearwater is similar. A considerable air-speed is a requisite of continuous gliding; albatrosses and shearwaters overtake, sail and soar around a fastmoving steamer without difficulty, and are seen to beat their wings seldom, and chiefly when, turning or mounting, they stall and lose momentum for a second or two.

The observer sees that they are able to accompany a ship without overtaking it too quickly only when it is steaming against the wind because their 'ground' speed is then reduced by the speed of the wind,

The albatross is legendary – this one is a black-browed albatross.

but they move too fast when a ship is steaming with the wind and must then make a series of ellipses far out to port and starboard if they would keep with the ship. In calm weather these long-winged petrels manoeuvre in all directions and their true flight-speed, estimated to reach at least sixty miles an hour, is then more easily gauged.

The flight track is always slightly curved, and although the albatross is seen to fly more often on a level keel than the smaller shearwater, both proceed by careering from side to side, rising up ten or twenty feet at the end of each movement to gain height (momentum is thereby lost) for the powerful downward plunge that shall carry the bird skimming at speed low over the surface of the sea. The observer sees first the dark back of the bird turned to him, and one wing-tip all but touching the crest or side or trough of the swell, then the bird rises, perhaps with one, or two, wing beats, swings slowly over, and presents the (usually) white belly to view as it glides gracefully onwards on the other tack. Once they have settled on a dead calm sea the albatrosses and the larger shearwaters have some difficulty in rising from the surface. When approached quickly in a boat, they flap awkwardly for a long distance over the surface, paddling with their legs, and may settle again without having got on the wing at all. If they are full fed they often lighten themselves by disgorging food. But in rough weather they easily launch themselves by opening their wings into the wind from the top of a wave, and are airborne immediately. On land they need a long run to take off in fine weather if they cannot drop into the air from a cliff or high rock, or unless a strong wind is blowing.

The flight of the shorter-winged fulmars is similar, but the gliding periods are shorter, and turning and banking manoeuvres are achieved within a narrower compass, the wings being broader and the primaries rather more flexible than those of the albatrosses and shearwaters.

Very different is the flight at sea of the storm-petrels and frigate-petrels, which is best described as an erratic bat-like flitting, with brief intervals of gliding. It has been called swallow-like, but it lacks the directness of the swallow's flight, though it is almost as fast, and the wings are more expanded and the whole motion more light and wavering. In rough as in calm weather these little petrels follow the undulations of swell and wave, keeping within a few inches of the heaving surface, with an astonishing nicety. It is only when feeding or searching for food that they hover, dropping their webbed feet to the surface, and paddling upon it lightly as if walking, and sometimes diving for a moment. The word petrel (according to most dictionaries) is derived from St Peter who walked the waves. The frigate- and Wilson's petrels use their long legs more often for this purpose and have an even more erratic flight. But these dainty petrels also dive well; we have seen storm-petrels at their best in wild weather off the Rockall Bank feeding and diving in the heavy swell. They would skim the marbled slopes of the sea, hesitate for a fraction of a second as they sighted food, then plunge under the surface for perhaps one, two or three seconds, scarcely folding their wings; and emerging with the same ease, wings swiftly spread, and every feather perfectly dry.

James Fisher's special favourite was the fulmar, his interest in which became an obsession. In 1952, he published a special study of the bird called *The Fulmar*.

On a still morning in early November some fulmars come back to their ocean-facing cliff. In ones and twos they fly silently up and down the rock-face, occasionally gliding over the cliff-top and making an overland excursion of a few yards. A group of twenty settles on the calm sea a hundred yards from the cliff-foot; they growl and cackle. From time to time a fulmar leaves the water-group and flies up to the cliff-face, to tour up and down. In the evening the wind gets up, and with it the sea; next morning the fulmars have gone. A week later it is calm again, and they are back; this time one settles on a ledge for a few minutes. All through December the number of visitors increases, though all disappear whenever the weather is stormy; many now land on ledges, and visit each other, display and cackle on them; on a fine day the cliff is decorated with fulmars alone, fulmars in twos, and fulmars (commonly) in threes. And so the situation continues; not long after Christmas, on a fine day when the temperature is nevertheless well below freezing-point, an observer may see some hundreds of fulmars on the cliffs, perhaps as many as half or two-thirds of (and sometimes actually more than) the population at the peak of the previous breeding-season.

Fisher expressed firm views on the reasons for the increase of the fulmar in recent decades.

There can be no possible doubt that the fulmar has evolved into a plankton-feeder, and that it normally searches for the larger plankton on which whales also feed, and eats it where it can be found; for instance, if and when it comes to the surface at night, or near icebergs or floes, or at the face of sea-running glaciers, or (at least in the North Atlantic) at a convergence of ocean currents or tides. The fulmar appears also to be a natural scavenger, and to eat any flesh, dung or blubber that it can get hold of. Probably it always shared in the dissection and dismemberment of dead whales floating at the surface, or stranded in shallow water. It is my thesis that the fulmar's spread began when whaling increased the population of dead whales in the fulmar's area; that this whaling enabled the fulmars to make a real change in their feeding-habits (but without starting something *entirely* new); and that, when whaling petered out, offshore trawling kept up a special food-supply - even more regularly than did whaling.

An ancient centre of the fulmar population, lying far to the west of the other islands of the Outer Hebrides, is St Kilda. Also in *The Fulmar*, Fisher describes it.

On the memorable still, clear days of the Western Isles an observer, resting at the top of a mountain of Lewis or Uist, or upon the Cuillin of Skye, or a high hill in the north of that island, may see St Kilda. It will be a dark nick, or two dark nicks, in the western sky. A fleecy cloud may trail away from it and mingle with other clouds, dark with rain to come. The high islands of Hirta and Soay and Boreray, which jut a quarter of a mile into the sky, will be weather-making. Often, when they are hull-down below the horizon, their cloud-scarf betrays their place: this is about forty-two miles west of the rest of the Outer Hebrides, and about 110 miles from the nearest point on the mainland of Scotland.

St Kilda, once the home of a brave human culture based on birds, is man's island no longer; deserted since 29 August 1930, it is now a natural sanctuary of wild life, which humans visit very seldom, and only as observers. The deserted village slowly decays; the stone store-chambers of the islanders silt up with the droppings of sheep, and the bones of those that go into them to die; St Kilda's big dark field-mice scuttle about the rotting floors of the houses and chew the pages of mouldy magazines in the corners of the rooms. Roof-slates drop, and gravestones topple. The wild animals possess the place.

The cliffs of St Kilda are mostly of a purplish-blue gabbro, with the chief exception of the height of Conachair and the cliffs of Hirta to the east of it, which are of granite, light in colour. They are much veined and stained by various minerals, and they are crowned with steep, much broken slopes and very green turf. Much turf grows on the buttresses and in the gullies of the cliffs, and in these steep places also grow dock and sorrel, and rose-root, and primroses. A thousand feet above the St Kilda sea, the primroses do not flower until late May or June, and the fulmars often sit on their nests among posies of flowers. Seen from a distance the brooding fulmars themselves look like flowers. At the east end of Conachair is a great projecting buttress, Ard Uachdarachd; it is possible to scramble down on to this from above, to a wild perch a thousand and fifty feet above the sea, and to survey from this perch almost the entire fulmar-slopes of Conachair. Here, on the green-covered cliffs, among scurvy-grass, angelica, polypody, shieldfern and the universal sheep's fescue, two thousand fulmar-flowers flourish.

The greatest concentration of nests on St Kilda in 1949 was on the three miles from the promontory of Gob na h-Airde (through which the sea has forced a great tunnel), east to the Point of Coll by the entrance of the Village Bay. This stretch includes the great cliffs of Conachair and Oiseval, and had nearly twelve thousand nests. There were over four thousand on the Cambir, the north-west peninsula of Hirta; and on Soay the 7500 nests were mostly on its dark north-west cliff (a sinister place which the evening sun can scarcely colour). There were 3600 nests on the Dùn and about 5600 on Boreray, though they were not so dense as on these other cliffs; and there were nearly four thousand nests on the long south-west cliffs of Hirta, though here they were in places

Pairs of fulmars cackle to each other at colonies all round Britain.

scattered, and grouped on the little precipices that crop through the steep grazing-slope of this part of the island.

All day, at the tops of all cliffs, the pale albatrosses of St Kilda play, and sway on the up-winds. From the Atlantic they slant their way a thousand feet up to their nests; at the level of these they become sail-planes and swing along the cliff-top, visiting their neighbours and watching them with cold dark eyes.

The fascinating spread of the fulmar, and all the evocative places with romantic-sounding names which it now occupies, were thoroughly documented by James Fisher in *The Fulmar*. Seton Gordon was also inspired by the charisma of this particular seabird, as this extract from *In Search of Northern Birds* (1941) shows.

There is a quality of grace and buoyancy in the fulmar's flight which is very unusual. The wings are sharp-pointed and are held stiffly and not bent at the joints like the wings of flying gulls. The swift glides remind me of the flight of a peregrine, but the fulmar in wind is more buoyant and airy than a peregrine, and in its sudden twists and turns, made without effort, it is unique. On this day of north wind, which blew in upon their cliff, the fulmars sailed happily backwards and forwards a few yards from the top of the precipice, rising and falling on wings that were held motionless. At times they uncannily checked their flight, remained almost without movement with scarcely a flutter of their wings, then spun round as though suspended by an invisible thread and moved by an invisible hand. During these flights the tail was constantly used to steer the flier, and the feet, which were usually held wide apart, with the legs in a slanting position, were sometimes used as auxiliary rudders. Although there were scores of fulmars in the air, many more were courting excitedly on the long green seas that swept in upon the coast and threatened to engulf them. Those birds swam facing one another, uttering hoarse quacking guttural cries, quickly repeated: some of the swimmers were bathing, flapping and drenching their wings in the sea which had been their home for at least four months, in storm and in fair weather.

A considerable proportion of the fulmar colony were squatting on the ledges where they would later lay. Like the razorbill and guillemot, the fulmar finds difficulty in walking in an upright position. The legs are scarcely strong enough to bear the bird's weight, and although the fulmar can, and indeed does, upon occasion walk upright it usually shuffles along on its knee joints, and when at rest always assumes a brooding attitude.

This scene of joy and activity at the fulmar cliff was delightful, for it showed that days of warmth and sunshine were surely approaching, when the plunging solan would send a fountain of spray into the warm air, and on ledges of the cliff primrose and sea thrift, roseroot and bird's foot trefoil would spread a gay carpet and scent the wayward June airs – when, across ocean haze, the hills of Wester Ross and Sutherland would rise nobly to the summer sky, and the gentle summer swell would break white upon the skirts of Trodday. Then the fulmar's flight would have lost something of its buoyancy, for it is a true child of the wind, and in calm, hot weather its wings must be driven to move it through the air. Some of the fulmars on the cliff that February day must have been immature birds, for there were fully twice as many pairs at the colony as I had seen in previous seasons. But that was to be expected, for it is a feature of any fulmar colony that a proportion of the birds frequent the nesting ledges during the spring, but lay no eggs.

The voice of the fulmar is also characteristic and an essential ingredient. Fisher sums it up in *The Fulmar* (1952).

If we place the components of these all together, in alphabetical order, we get something a little nearer the fantastic, ecstatic sound that a trio of fulmars, displaying on (or signalling or "discussing" the ownership of) a nest-site, can produce: *aaark – ag – ah – ak – arrr – brrae – buck – caw – cok – coo – eck – ga – gä – gaggeragaggagagga – gagagagaga – gah – gerrr – grorr – grrr – ha – haw – hough – i – kaka – karo – kekerek – kertchük – kokokok – kraw – kuh – kurr – kwakwakwa – oh – ok – ork – r – rherrrrrr – roo – tchück – uä – ug – uh – uk – urg – urk – wib.* In 1948, in Shetland, Ludwig Koch recorded the voices of some fulmars on a series of gramophone discs. He waited hours to get the birds at a suitable pitch of emotion, and finally recorded a *crescendo* of cawing, croaking, rolling throaty sounds which must be heard to be believed; certainly this composite, of all that the voices of the fulmar have been represented to be, gets as near to it as seems possible.

The voice of the fulmar can, then, be described, rather feebly but fairly accurately, as a cackling. This cackling is heard where fulmars feed and breed. On the nest-ledges it is heard at every pitch of intensity – from a quiet crooning to an orgasm of vocal excitement – and with every variation that the combination of the consonants c, g, h, k, q and r can produce, and others besides. At sea (except below the breeding-cliffs) it is seldom heard, for fulmars appear to be silent when feeding alone – unless a school of fulmars is following the offal and slick of a fishing-boat or whaler; then the denser the school, the louder the noise – "like frogs", wrote Martens the whaler.

A close relative of the fulmar is the Manx shearwater. Ronald Lockley studied this bird on the island of Skokholm off the coast of Dyfed, and wrote of the experience in his book called simply *Shearwaters* (1942).

Man is accustomed to think and speak of the sea-birds plurally, lumping them together in flocks, hosts, crowds, and so on. Certainly it was easy for me to do this in the case of the Manx shearwater. Before I came to Skokholm I had only seen the bird in flocks off the coasts of Lundy Island in the Bristol Channel. There they had all been flying north towards Skokholm and Skomer, their great breeding ground in the west. I have never been able to find out whether the Manx shearwater breeds on Lundy, but lighthouse keepers have assured me that they have often heard the birds "singing" at night there, and occasionally they have found a nest. It may be that, as in the Isle of Man, where the species was first named, they have more or less abandoned Lundy on account of the rats which infest that island. Howbeit, after those flocks off Lundy, and a night with the shearwaters at Skomer, the sister island lying two miles or so north of Skokholm, I suddenly found myself master of this island of Skokholm and its ten thousand pairs of shearwaters.

Ten thousand. That was my first rough estimate of their numbers on Skokholm's 242 acres. In the day-time all you saw of them was a sprinkling of corpses at the rate of about six to the acre over the whole island. These unlucky ones had been slain by the great black-backed gulls and were now no more than inverted skins – perhaps, if the gull had been voracious, only wings and breast-bone.

But on dark nights in the spring and summer the shearwaters appeared, coming out from their holes in the ground and joining together in a bedlam of weird screaming. There seemed at first no intelligence in that wild howling – it was the crying of insane spirits wandering without aim or restraint over the rough rocks and the bare pastures. Indeed I cannot now properly describe that noise of the shearwater. I once got some friends to write on slips of paper what they considered was a phonetic rendering of a typical individual scream of the Manx shearwater. We then exchanged slips and each read aloud the other's rendering. The result was amusing but unconvincing. Then we tried similes. "Like the crow of a throaty rooster whose head is chopped off before the last long note has fairly begun," was judged the best. And I will leave it at that.

Manx shearwaters take on a special air of mystery because they visit their colonies only at night. Lockley continues, describing a night in the colony.

It is difficult to follow the nocturnal movements of the shearwaters. They arrive in what to man is darkness, and, preferring the black night, they are naturally not prepared to perform their business under the flood-light of the observer's torch. This must be used discreetly. How often, when with the shearwaters at night, have I not longed for the eyes of a cat or an owl! I was going to add, and best of all, the eyes of a shearwater; but my study of the bird has taught me to be cautious. The eye of the shearwater is surprisingly small, a little chocolate disk no larger than the head of a blue-bottle, or the head of Britannia on a penny. Such a small eye is obviously more adapted for making use of the brilliant light of the sun reflected from the surface of the sea, on and over which most of the shearwater's life is spent. While in the complete darkness of the shearwater's burrow the most sensitive eye in the world is not of much use. The bird in the burrow seems to manage very well by employing the other senses, those of touch, hearing, and, as it has nostrils, we can confidently add, smell.

But we are going too fast. We left the home-coming shearwater in the air, flying over a great honeycomb of rabbit burrows, in one of which, if it is a female bird, it will presently lay an egg. That we know as a fact, but whether, having laid an egg, the bird will incubate it or leave this work to its mate, or perhaps even to another shearwater, we do not know. Sea-birds, if you study them long enough, reveal such unconventional habits that it is not safe to assign to them any accepted patterns of behaviour as laid down in text-books on birds. And the Manx shearwater has never been studied in the field.

Let us for a moment imagine ourselves to be a shearwater flying in to Skokholm from the sea. We have had a long day skimming the sea, feeding on small fishes and surface-swimming crustacean life, and now we are anxious to be home and busy about nesting affairs. As we cannot nest in the sphere best known to us, the wind and the sea, we had chosen the next thing, an island, which, surrounded by wind and sea, yet has the necessary stable foundation of rock and earth to burrow in.

Manx shearwaters spend most of their life skimming the waves.

For centuries our forbears have dug their holes in its surface, and like the ancestors of man have, by their pioneering, made our lot easier. We have in fact only to alight on the island to find a ready-made hole.

But consider: the night is pitch dark, and below us there is not one hole but a thousand, indeed a hundred thousand, holes, a honeycomb which will not bear the weight of human foot without the crust giving way. How shall we, humans in birds' skins, discover our particular hole in an acre of such flat and featureless ground? At least it looks flat and featureless, this village city of the birds, where all homes are alike and there are neither streets nor directing notices. Here and there are outcrops of rock from which we might take rough bearings, if we could see them in the dark. These outcrops might help us to narrow our search somewhat, but could not guide us accurately to the chosen hole.

It was darker now. The scent of the bluebells came to me in a gust of

57

wind. They are nearly perfect at this hour of May, leaping up in the recent rains, thick and strong of stem, sun and wind kissed, deep purple, heavy with bells, unlike your pale fragile attenuated woodland blooms. Here on the knoll they have adventured across the grass far from the bracken. As a rule they grow on the island chiefly in association with this fern which, springing up after the bluebells have flowered, provides the shade and moisture which the bulbs need for a full maturity.

Suddenly I heard the first cry of the shearwater on the wing, afar off on the edge of the wind. A wild cry, but softened by distance and lent enchantment by a new knowledge of what it signified, a cry I was beginning to understand at last. Almost at once Ada, in the burrow close at my feet, answered. But no, it was not her mate Adam – it was too much to expect that of the ten thousand homing shearwaters Adam would be first.

The voice in the distance faded – the bird had turned away to the west of the island before the last screech. In the interval before the next I heard a whistling, a rippling note – whimbrel flying north to the Shetlands, the Faeroes, and Iceland. And then the gaggling of a skein of geese, a rare noise on this rocky western coast. I could hear the hiss of wings coming up from the south louder and louder, then slowly dying away north of me. But it was too dark to see anything – perhaps they were white-fronted geese bound for the ice-covered tundra of Spitsbergen.

Soon after 10 p.m. (by Greenwich mean time), with the whole island resounding with the wild screams of the shearwaters, Adam arrived with a piercing yell and crashed with a distinct thump upon the turf right in front of his burrow. He rested there for a second or so. Ada immediately squawked, saying as plainly as a shearwater may: "Come inside, quick!" And Adam waddled in straight away. The light of my torch just caught his extremities – tail, legs, and wing-tips – as they vanished through the rather narrow entrance hole.

Now ensued a domestic scene which can only be imagined from the cooing and cackling that followed. I crept nearer the burrow and laid my ear to the ground above the nesting recess. The noise seemed to shake the burrow, and though it came up out of the earth as it were, it was quite unearthly. Similar meetings and greetings were going on in the other burrows, soft pedal to the wild night anthem of the island. I cannot describe even phonetically the individual notes of Adam and his wife. They were, I suppose, variations of the typical triple shout of the species. Yet it seemed to me that these variations had something of the intelligibility of spoken words. At one moment they seemed to be discussing the amazing new egg, at the next they were apparently billing and cooing, and probably, from the rising pitch of their excited duet, mating. There was movement as well as talk. But increasing intervals of quietude followed, punctuated briefly, perhaps, by an occasional sharp squeak. And from time to time the deafening duet.

A smaller petrel (indeed the smallest of our seabirds) is the storm petrel. The closely similar Leach's petrel is not much bigger. Kenneth Williamson enjoyed studying them in the Faeroes. Here is an extract from *The Atlantic Islands* (1948).

Petrels are the sparrows of the sea, abundant little birds who roam far on tireless wings between horizons of uneasy, volatile waves. The sea is one of the richest feeding-grounds on this planet, and they and numerous allied creatures have fitted themselves for a life that has no need of land, except as a place where they can perpetuate the species. So they nest on the fringe of the ocean, often on remote and isolated islets. There may be thousands nesting on Mykineshólmur but you would never know it unless you looked for them at night: for while the sun shines they must reap their harvest far from any land, and it is only when the night comes that they go in the stillness to the lonely shores where their nesting-tunnels are scored in the soil.

A night with the petrels is a remarkable and memorable event. Two kinds nest in the west of Mykines and the holm – the storm, more romantically known as "Mother Carey's Chicken," and the rather larger and browner Leach's forked-tailed petrel. Because of the comparative isolation and inaccessibility of its few known breeding-places, Leach's petrel is one of the special treasures of a bird-watcher's life. How many there are on Mykineshólmur and that western peninsula I do not know and cannot guess with any degree of confidence. Salomonsen recorded that in 1934 the species was a newcomer to the Faeroes and only four or five pairs were nesting. Either it had been previously overlooked, or its increase since that year has been phenomenal, for its population to-day cannot be less than as many thousand pairs.

The summer night is alive with these elfin birds, shadows a shade darker than the sky flitting to and fro in a whirl of giddy movement. They electrify the air, dancing around like strange, nocturnal butterflies, and with the same wayward flight as big-winged, exotic butterflies. One moment a dozen are visible whilst you watch, and the next moment they are gone with the gloom. They swirl and eddy about your head, sometimes brushing past your face with a soft, ghostly touch. The night is feverish with brisk, excited movement and their clear staccato cries; for they are constantly calling, and their eerie voices are flung against the murmur of the wave-roll on the shore and the soft sweep of the wind through the long grass. It is an unreal and fascinating world which any naturalist would feel pride and joy in visiting for a while.

When the last pale wash of sunset is in the sky the storm petrels come to the isle. They are the first to arrive. The path on the northern side of Rógvukollur is a good place to see them, and in parts of west Mykines they outnumber the larger kind. The old ruin on the south-east corner of the holm is another of their strongholds, and here they fly in wide circles, fast and fairly direct, and in the gloaming their quaint conversation and mysterious love-making begins. Their song rises out of the earth or comes from among the stones of the ruined walls; it is a thin, whirring song reminiscent of the hum of a spinning-wheel. The Leach's petrels are later in their arrival, but soon after dark they are to be found fluttering in scores above the sloping brow where the pasture descends to the south side rocks, whilst one can also find them, though not in the same large numbers, on the brink of the great northern cliff. One of the finest vantage-points for watching both species, and the Manx shearwater as well, is on the lower side of Klettur. On Mykines itself the Leach's flies thickly above the Lambi *lundaland* and extends as far eastwards as Dalid and the north-west cliff behind the village *bour*.

We "fleyged" the petrels with the fowling-net; or, it is more truthful to say, my companion "fleyged" and I watched, and was kept amused by his antics whilst awaiting opportunities to use my rings. Sofus Sivertsen has great skill with the *fleyg*, but he met his Waterloo that night on the teeming holm. He danced and shouted like a Dervish in the dusky light, his accustomed calm and quiet confidence completely shattered by the will- o' -the-wisp tactics of these astonishing sprites. When the net was passed to me for a spell I merely floundered of little purpose, breathing heavily from the unusual exertion, and feeling much pity for the aching muscles of my arms. I too loudly deplored the birds' nimble ways, their loud cackle of a cry that seemed to mock my clumsy efforts, and their covering cloak of night, an ally and impervious retreat.

In actual fact we both caught more than we were able to hold in the net, for the birds are so quick and sprightly on the wing that the net never seemed to strike them with any force, and only a few became sufficiently entangled to find escape impossible. Many merely brushed

The storm petrel is the smallest of our seabirds.

against the strands and shot away again before we could effect their capture. The *fleygaslong* was much too heavy for the fast, close work required; something lighter and easier to wield, say a ten-foot bamboo rod attached to a net of a smaller mesh, would be a great improvement. When I went home to breakfast later that morning my host grinned widely and said he supposed we had made history, for it must surely be the first time *drunnhviti* had been "fleyged" in the Faeroe Isles!

A simple translation of *drunnhviti* is "white rump," a feature common to both species, but having in the Leach's an admixture of brown feathers extending downwards from the middle of the back. The name really belongs to the storm petrel: few of the Mykines people are able to distinguish between the two, which is not surprising if the species now dominating the holm has only nested there since 1934.

In *Island Years* (1940), Frank Fraser Darling notes the arrival of the storm petrels for the breeding season on his Hebridean island.

I never cease from wonder at the storm petrel and its life. How does it manage to survive and increase? Think of a bird of such small size and slender build living from October to June on the face of the mighty ocean, never coming to land. Perhaps the very smallness of its bulk saves it from being buffeted, so that it walks the waves in freedom or sits on them as lightly as a cork.

They come to us about the 2nd of June and occupy the ruins of the outlaw's house, the cletts on the ramp of storm beach near the west landing, little stretches of dyke on the east side of the island, the tumble of fallen rocks below the central ridge and any rickle of boulders almost anywhere on the island which will give them a dry place. I have even found one in a crack of the peat in the middle of the island. The birds come in the night and only betray their presence by their churring song, which goes on and on, sometimes night and day as well. We have found this sound to have a restful and comforting quality.

One of these mites nested in an accessible place in the outlaw's shieling, so that we were able to take an occasional look at her and her egg. One large white egg, an egg often cold and taking five weeks to hatch; then a helpless chick, it also often left for a period of days without feeding and taking three months to fledge, a chick which receives no after-care from its parents, but which is just left in the dark and bare cavern where it was hatched. It must come forth into the world of its own initiative and face the stormy environment of the ocean in autumn. What a tenuous thread is this for the survival of the species! We have no knowledge of what the death-rate may be during their life on the ocean; probably it is low, but each year that the adult birds come to land to breed is a time of danger and loss. On Clerach the otters take a grievous toll, and I often find a head, and tail and legs, lying a piteous relic near an otter's lair. These birds find their worst enemy in the great black-backed gull on North Rona, though I cannot understand how this wretch manages to catch them. You find the remains of the petrels in the casts of the black-backs.

The storm petrel is the smallest of our seabirds – in stark contrast to the gannet, which is our biggest. Bryan Nelson introduces the bird, and his marvellous book *The Gannet* (1978) shows that a modern monograph can still contain brilliantly evocative writing, born of acute, perceptive and appreciative observation.

By cautious movement one can penetrate to the heart of a gannetry without disturbing it. There, from gannet's eye level, and without the protective capsule of space, it becomes faintly possible to imagine what it may feel like to be a site-owning gannet in a great colony. You are encircled with bayonets, steely beaks boldy outlined in black and couched between cold blue eyes. Serried ranks of birds guard their drums, snowy plumage stirring in the wind. In early July some are still neatly on top of the mould, sealing the nest-cup as they incubate stained eggs; others are brooding reptilian squabs or standing guard over fluffy chicks already approaching adult size; a few stand on empty, flattened pads or even bare sites. Rare indeed is the unguarded site, whatever its contents, and if it is evening, many nests hold pairs. If this sounds a peaceful scene, nothing could be further from the truth. The noise and activity is phenomenal. You are engulfed by waves of brassy sound. The air is thick with gannets, signalling their arrival with harsh incoming calls, or fishing low over the nesting mass, stimulating outbursts of display. From single birds, sweeping movements with heraldically outspread wings and rhythmic bows, and from re-united pairs, ecstatic meeting ceremonies. Over all, the metallic clangour that, in unison, and at some distance, is the full-throated uproar of a great gannetry. Indeed, a gannet city so far as crowds and stimulus go, but in no sense chaotic. In fact, the two most prominent and thought-provoking features of a gannetry are the tempo of activity and the rigidly ordered framework within which it occurs.

Ronald Lockley visited the Grassholm colony, which has since grown vastly greater. He describes it in *I Know an Island* (1938).

A great clamour was coming to us from the direction of the gannets on the north-west cliffs out of our sight. A good whiff of stale fish drifted to us too. We could see the moulted fragments of white down from the growing young gannets, a kind of snowstorm floating high in the air above us or slowly sinking into the windless cove where we lay so comfortably, our backs to the warm rock. Pieces of this airy down settled in our hair, on our clothes, even upon our food.

We were now in the right mood to start our tour of the island. At one time myriads of puffins inhabited Grassholm. To-day a mere handful is left. The whole of this south ravine of Grassholm is brown and bare, a sunbaked Pompeii of the first puffin invasion, for only the turf walls of the puffin township remain, the roofs having collapsed under stress of winter storms and the birds' undermining work. Walking across the ruins was difficult: your foot slipped two or three feet down into passages between the quaking turf ridges. We struggled across this maze to the highest rock of the island. From this point the gannets are spread below you like some rare ballet in blue and silver and gold.

It is impossible for me to describe as it deserves to be described that sight of ten thousand or so big white birds spaced so closely and evenly over two acres of sloping ground. Each bird, or pair of birds, was guarding a hummock crowned with a nest of seaweed and dead grass, and each bird was as beautiful to look at as the whole colony itself, the white head tinged with golden yellow, the bill plumbeous and bayonet-like, the eye pale as silver, the plumage snow-white except for the black wing-tips, and the legs and the toes of the webbed feet black with unreal longitudinal stripes of blue-green. In each nest was a single young bird, a ball of white down from which protruded black beak and feet. Here and there was an unhatched egg or a youngster with the black juvenile feathers well grown. Overhead was a great wheel of thousands of gannets moving steadily northward over the colony, then turning southward over the sea to complete the circle. The wing-spread of a gannet must be nearly six feet. The great squadron sailed close over our heads, each individual glancing down at us with those cold but human-looking eyes, with golden head bent and bill pointed at us.

A jumble of idle thoughts came to me as we sat watching the gannets – wonder at the beauty of the scene and wonder that since the gannets seem to nest together on the principle of safety in numbers the birds did

A gannet colony is a memorable place – full of life and atmosphere.

not combine to attack intruders. The bills and wings of a thousand gannets could have finished us very quickly. But though there was a great clatter going on, like the talk of nations upset by some outrage affecting them all, nothing was done about it, and when I went to look at the chick in the nearest nest only the bird in possession stood to defend it. So that I, as a powerful aggressor, could do my worst with the screaming individual.

This adult gannet lunged at me with its sharp bill. Then as I reached out to take the nestling it made a pumping motion with its neck and suddenly threw up from its crop a mackerel, fairly fresh and with only the head partly digested. Thus lightened, with a final clatter of protest it blundered away into the wind. The young bird copied its parent to the point of throwing up a half-digested squid. But it was too young to do more than stand in the nest and make feeble passes at my hand.

Other birds were being sick to left and right as a result of my presence. Being sick in this way is an instinctive reaction; induced possibly by fear, it serves to lighten the bird and makes a getaway easier.

It seemed a pity to let all these birds lose their lunches. So we backed out of the colony, thinking that they would re-swallow their fish messes. But they never tried to, and, indeed, they got very little chance. The herring-gulls and great black-backed gulls dropped down with greedy cries at our heels and gobbled all these savoury bits warm from the crop. The gannets could have killed these gulls, but once again only individual action was taken, each gannet defending its nest only and not troubling about the fish thrown down beside it. One great black-backed gull finished off his fish meal by swallowing whole a naked new-hatched gannet chick out of a nest from which the parent gannet had been driven by our approach.

Nowadays, birdwatchers would not risk being the cause of such predation and disturbance of breeding gannets should be avoided. In *Seabirds* (1954), Fisher and Lockley discuss the fishing methods of gannets.

The food and fishing methods of the gannets have been well described by Gurney (1913), who concludes that the deeper the fish are swimming the higher the altitude from which the gannet's plunge is made. He records that the Belfast fishermen are thereby guided as to the depths at which to set their nets. There is generally a mistaken notion that the gannet dives in order to gain impetus and strength to *spear* its prey; and the story is handed down of how trawler hands tie a fish on to a piece of floating wood so as to deceive the gannet, which is killed by the impact of its dive upon the board, or else – more popular report still – its bill is embedded in the wood. These tales are largely without foundation in fact; one trawlerman told us that every time he tried this experiment of tying a fish to a board and trailing it astern when gannets were present, the fish was devoured by other birds which alighted beside the floating wood. The gannet does not spear the fish: the dive is for the purpose of gaining depth and velocity under water in order to attack a fish or shoal *from beneath,* and the fish is seized in the open bill as the bird rises to the surface. It is usually swallowed under water, unless it is large; gannets are sometimes attacked and pursued in the air by skuas, and boobies are chased by man-o'-war birds; and it is probably from fear of these and of fellow competitors (Kay, 1948) that the gannet and booby swallow as much of their fish-food as possible under water. Having done so, however they are by no means free from the air attacks of the skuas (great, arctic and pomarine skuas are recorded as attacking the gannet), and man-o'-war birds, which will often pursue them until they are forced to disgorge. Some skuas, particularly the great skua, will tenaciously follow a gannet which has been feeding, and several reliable observers have reported that the skua has grabbed the tail of the gannet in its determination to force the gannet to throw up.

In *The Gannet* (1978), Bryan Nelson's scientific appraisal of their feeding habits makes absorbing reading.

We know little about the actual mechanics of prey capture. First, the gannet obviously does see its quarry before it plunges, and tracks it all the way down. The exquisite manoeuvrings are evidence of this. Most likely, the gannet takes its deeper prey on the way down, by which time it will have re-oriented and begun pursuit; or on the way up if its prey is near the surface. Gannets do not dive with their beaks open and it would hardly be possible to open them whilst still under the full impetus of a powerful plunge, in other words whilst still near the surface. Shallow dives may be of this kind, a plunge being followed by a rapid turn and an attempted capture. Sometimes gannets undoubtedly spear large fish, and indeed a gannet was recovered with the carcase of a puffin round its neck! It has been suggested that the terrific impact of a full-blooded dive stuns fish which are just below the surface, the blow being transmitted by the water rather than absorbed, and Barlee has himself stunned a large pike by hitting the water with an oar.

In addition to plunging, gannets have been recorded swimming among fry and scooping them up; fishing on foot in shallow, sandy bays, presumably for sand-eels; and diving from the surface and pursuing fish by swimming with strokes of half-opened wings, as does the brown booby. Booth's captive gannets dived from the surface in a manner closely resembling the plunge made by a coot.

Although gannets often hunt singly, they are undoubtedly communal feeders, congregating in masses, up to a thousand or more, typically above shoals of herring or mackerel. Contrary to what one might suppose, the conspicuous white plumage of the gannet is not merely an inadvertent 'marker'. A gannet does not give the show away, and attract others, because it cannot hide its plunges. On the contrary, the dazzling plumage, as Darwin remarked, is a positive attractant. Gannet plumage has evolved because it is an advantage to the diving bird to attract others to the spot, and attract them it certainly does. Many observers relate the dramatic way in which a fishing flock crystallises and grows, the birds streaming in from every side. The signaller, as well as the responder, derives benefit from communal fishing. Shoals of fish that are subjected to a continuous hailstorm of diving gannets probably become fragmented, disoriented, confused, and greatly fatigued by frequent use of their rapid-swim muscles, thus falling an easier prey to each gannet than if the latter were hunting on its own. It is a question of helping oneself by helping one's neighbour; the latter is not acting as a competitor in the ultimate sense, even if he is going for the same shoal. It is understandable, therefore, that selection pressure has favoured the evolution of the most advertant plumage (as indeed the gannet's is) and the response of conspecifics to it. Furthermore, it is not surprising that under these circumstances gannets often have the chance to "gorge themselves silly". It is "fortunate" that this is exactly what they are morphologically equipped to do, with fat-banks to replenish against lean days, and greatly demanding young to feed in record time!

When in full cry, they become hysterically active. The splash of a lobbed stone will precipitate simultaneous plunges from several birds and as the frenzy grows, the living projectiles rain down within inches of each other, or of boats. Nor do they always miss the boats. They may dive into nets full of fish, into scuppers, onto decks, into holds – even, it is recorded, into a fish-curing shed in Penzance. Most ringing recoveries at sea are from birds handled by fishermen. In full spate, it is no wonder that some will be fooled by a fish tied to a board, and break their necks, as fisherman traditionally relate since before Martin Martin visited the St Kildans. In fiction, L. A. G. Strong, in *The Brothers*, caused one brother to murder the other by having him towed along in the water with a fish tied to his forehead, tempting gannets to do the rest. There is even a recent record of a gannet following a plough, with a cloud of gulls, near Lochgilphead. Doubtless the sight of the gulls and the beat of a diesel engine triggered Trawler-scavenging behaviour in the gannet. They quickly become conditioned to the noise of lifting gear on boats and will join a boat in response to this before there are any fish to be seen.

Seton Gordon watched gannets at the Butt of Lewis and recaptures the moment in *In Search of Northern Birds* (1941).

At the Butt two flight-lines of gannets converge – the flight-lines of birds nesting on St Kilda, 60 miles to the west, and of those which have their home upon Sùla Sgeir, just under 40 miles to the north. For long I stood on the promontory and watched these passing solans. From the south came flight after flight of these strong winged birds, all making their way north a short distance off the east coast of Lewis. These travellers rounded the Butt and, with a wind that was now fair to them on their altered course, steered south-west for distant St Kilda where a vast colony of the species have their summer home. From the south-west, also, flying in the teeth of the breeze, parallel to the west coast of Lewis and about 100 yards off shore, came many other solans. The majority of these travellers flew high, but a proportion of them made their way only a foot or two above the surface of the waves, moving heavily as though gorged with fish. These low-flying birds were evidently solans nesting on Sùla Sgeir and were returning home from the fishing grounds: they continued on their course beyond the Butt in the direction of that ocean rock. But the high-flying gannets did not accompany those flying just above the ocean's surface: these rounded the Butt in a stately manner, then flew south into the Minch, steering towards the large fishing fleet from Stornoway which could be seen, before sunset, searching for herring shoals. These gannets were, I have little doubt, birds from St Kilda, making a long flight to fishing grounds in the Minch. The passing and repassing of the solan flights made a memorable picture. Each bird drove itself forward on strong, narrow wings at deceptive speed, moving always without a trace of hurry. The May sunlight glinted on white black-tipped wings, moving with rhythm. The birds passed singly, in little companies, sometimes in large flocks. Occasionally a flight passed almost over my head, but most of the birds kept some little distance out from the surfbeaten rocks. The solans were intent upon their journeying, and all that day I saw but one of them plunge beneath the green waters to snatch a fish during its flight.

In his book *The Land's End* (1908), W. H. Hudson speaks of the movement of gannets, and captures their character to perfection.

I have watched the Gannets passing by the hour, travelling to some distant feeding area or to their breeding haunts in the far north; a procession many a league long, but a very thin procession of twos and twos, every bird with his mate, following the trend of the coast, each bird in turn now above the sea, now down in the shelter of a big incoming wave, and every curve and every rise and fall of one so exactly repeated by the other as to give the idea of a bird and its shadow or reflection, with bird and reflection continually changing places.

Auks are some of the most important birds in the exciting scene of a busy seabird city. Edmund Selous watched them in Shetland, and gives his impressions in *The Birdwatcher in the Shetlands* (1905).

Oh, is there anything in life more piquant (if you care about it) than to lie on the summit of a beetling cliff, and watch the breeding sea-fowl on the ledges below? In the Shetlands, at least, it is possible to do this in perfect safety, for the strata of the rock have often been tilted up to such an extent that, whilst the precipice formed by their broken edges is of the most fearful description, their slope, even on the landward side, is so steep that when one has climbed it, and flung oneself full length at the top, one's head looks down – as mine does now – as from a slanting wall, against which one's body leans. To fall over, one would first have to fall upwards, and the knowledge of this gives a feeling of security, without which one could hardly observe or take notes. The one danger lies in becoming abstracted and forgetting where one is. Those steep, green banks – for the rock, except in smooth, unclimbable patches, is covered with lush grass – have no appearance of an edge, and I have often shuddered, whilst plodding mechanically upwards, to find myself but just awakened from a reverie, within a yard or so of their soft-curled, lap-like crests. But I think my "subliminal," in such cases, was always pretty well on the watch, or – to adopt a more prosaic and now quite obsolete explanation – the reverie was not a very deep one.

At any rate, here I am safe, and, looking down again from my old "coign of vantage" of two years before, the same wonderful and never forgotten – never-to-be-forgotten – sight presents itself. Here are the guillemots, the same individual birds, standing – each in the old place, perhaps, if the truth were known – in long, gleaming rows and little salient clusters, equally conspicuous by their compact shape and vividly contrasted colouring; whilst both above and below them, on nests which look like some natural, tufted growth of the sheer, jagged rock, and which touch, or almost touch, one another, sit hundreds and hundreds of kittiwakes, the soft bluey-grey and downier white of whose plumage, with their more yielding and accommodating outlines, make them as a tone and tinting of the rock itself, and delight with grace, as the others do with boldness. Seen from a distance all except the white is lost, and then they have the effect of snow, covering large surfaces of the hard, perpendicular rock. Nearer, they look like little nodules or bosses of snow projecting from a flatter and less pure expanse of it. An innumerable cry goes up, a vociferous, shrieking chorus, the sharp and ear-piercing treble to the deep, sombrous bass of the waves. The actual note is supposed to be imitated in the name of the bird, but to my own ear it much more resembles – to a degree, indeed, approaching exactitude – the words "It's getting late!" uttered with a great emphasis on the "late," and repeated over and over again in a shrill, harsh, and discordant shriek. The effect – though this is far from being really the case – is as though the whole of the birds were shrieking out this remark at the same time. There is a constant clang and scream, an eternal harsh

Most great seabird colonies have guillemots playing a major role.

music – harmony in discord – through and above which, dominating it as an organ does lesser instruments – or like "that deep and dreadful organ-pipe, the thunder" – there rolls, at intervals, one of the most extraordinary voices, surely, that ever issued from the throat of a bird: a rolling, rumbling volume of sound, so rough and deep, yet so full, grand, and sonorous, that it seems as though the very cliffs were speaking – ending sometimes in something like a gruff laugh, or, as some will have it, a bark.

This marvellous note is the nuptial one of the guillemot, or, rather, it is that, swelled and multiplied by the echoes to which it gives rise, and which roll and mutter along the face of the precipice, and mingle with the dash of the waves. The effect is most striking when heard at a little distance, and especially across the chasm that divides one precipice from another. Under these circumstances it is less the actual cry itself than what, by such help, it becomes, that impresses one.

In *A Fauna of the Outer Hebrides* (1888) Harvie-Brown and Buckley described a bird never to be seen again, the extinct great auk.

To repeat all the history of the Garefowl or Great Auk to some may not seem necessary, after the exhaustive accounts by Professor Newton, Gray, and the later publication of Mr Symington Grieve, but the following abstract of, or extracts from, their works may prove interesting, and preserve the continuity of our volume, as belonging entirely to St Kildian and O. Hebridean records. The account here given has been repeatedly told to tourist visitors and ornithologists visiting St Kilda. We ourselves, when we visited St Kilda in 1879, devoted more of our attention to a survey of the island, spending our short four hours on shore in endeavouring to see as much of it as possible, and ascending Connachar; and in this way we did not interview the old St Kildian personally on that occasion; but the tale told by him to Mr Boyd and other listeners varies little from the accounts given at later dates to other people by the same individual. We are obliged to Professor Newton for condensing the accounts, and the following is very nearly the exact contents of a letter we have received from him upon the subject.

"The bird, frightened by men on the cliff, jumped into a boat in which was a boy of fourteen years of age, named Donald MacQueen, whose son of the same name – now a man of from fifty to fifty-five years of age – gave Mr [Henry] Evans these particulars, and heard his father

Sadly extinct, the great auk must have been a remarkable sight.

say he caught the bird thus. It was on the main island, i.e. St Kilda itself.

"But it also seems, from Mr Evans' information, that another bird was caught on Stack-an-Armine, in or about 1840, by some five men who were stopping there for a few days. Three of them were Lauchlan McKinnon, about thirty years of age – and now, or till recently, alive – his father-in-law, and the elder Donald MacQueen before mentioned – both now dead. McKinnon told Mr Evans that they found the bird on a ledge of rock, that they caught it asleep, tied its legs together, took it up to their bothy, kept it alive for three days, and then killed it with a stick, *thinking it might be a witch.* They threw the body behind the bothy and left it there. McKinnon described the bird to Mr Evans, so that the latter has no doubt about its having been a Garefowl.

"It was Malcolm McDonald who actually laid hold of the bird, and held it by the neck with his two hands, till others came up and tied its legs. It used to make a great noise, like that made by a gannet, but much louder, when shutting its mouth. It opened its mouth when any one came near it. It nearly cut the rope with its bill. A storm arose, and that, together with the size of the bird and the noise it made, *caused them to think it was a witch*. It was killed on the third day after it was caught, and McKinnon declares they were beating it for an hour with two large stones before it was dead: he was the most frightened of all the men, and advised the killing of it. The capture took place in July. The bird was about halfway up the Stack. ('This last statement,' says Professor Newton, 'is, to me, conclusive that the bird could not have been a Great Northern or other Diver, as some have suggested.') That side of the Stack slopes up, so that a man can fairly easily walk up. There is grass upon it, and a little soil up to the point where they found the bird. Mr Evans says that he knows there is a good ledge of rock at the sea-level, from which a bird might start to climb to the place. Mr Evans tried in vain to fix the *exact* year in which this event happened, but could only get 1840 as an approximate estimate."

Of all the auks, puffins are perhaps the most written about and the most popular birds for beginners to watch. Kenneth Williamson describes in *The Atlantic Islands* (1948) seeing them in the Faeroes.

It is good to sit and watch the multitudes of birds going urgently about their daily tasks. Small crowds of them rise from the rocky ground before you, going off to the shining sea with a great rush of air from their vibrating wings. Sometimes, of course, it is your approach which causes this flurried movement, but even if you sit quietly in some inconspicuous place you will see similar communal behaviour among the scattered groups. One second the birds are standing together outside their burrows, doing nothing in particular, and the next - as though each bird had been visited by the same idea in the very same moment - the flock is scudding through the air to the puffin-dappled water below. When you gaze out to sea black spots dance in your vision, as in an attack of giddiness, but resolve themselves as your eyes focus into the distant mites of this vast horde of birds who spend the one half of their lives here on the ocean fringe.

Ronald Lockley devoted a whole book to the subject of puffins (*Puffins*, 1953), and colourfully describes all aspects of their behaviour. Here they are returning to their island.

The fleet is in! The flotillas of the puffins have anchored in the bays

73

and creeks of the islands. As if a toy armada of painted ships had suddenly and simultaneously come up from the sea-bed, we find them one morning, a day or two after the first scouts were seen, carpeting the quiet water at the base of their breeding cliffs.

Make haste to observe them; for from our experience of many years' study we know that to-morrow there may not be a puffin within sight of the islands. But it turns out that on this first day very little activity is observed. The puffins have appeared all at once, at about nine in the morning, in thousands. Their arrival had been unostentatious, an impression heightened by their silence. So idle are they, floating gently, hardly swimming at all, that one wonders if they are not perhaps tired, as if from a long journey? They sleep much, bill tucked back into the feathers at the base of the wing. Now and then one bird swims tentatively towards another or follows, or appears to follow, and guard a mate. They meet, rub bills together as if in greeting, then drift apart. There is a constant glancing towards the land, as if the puffins were anxious to go ashore; but this may be pure imagination on our part – a puffin never ceases when awake to swing its head in a half-circle, to and fro, a jerk at a time.

But no, the risk of going ashore is not taken on this first day. After two or three hours of inspecting the land, the sky, the water, and each other, the puffins suddenly depart without touching the land, moving away as quietly as they appeared, and vanish completely from the neighbourhood of the islands.

Lockley also studied the young birds, and even coined a delightful name for them.

Just before midnight the first puffling walked out of its burrow and made straight for the sea. There was very little hesitation. As if it had finished with all deliberation over making this tremendous voyage, it moved briskly to the water. It tumbled over small rocks and other obstacles, reached the slight cliff, and whirred down on stumpy wings. It struck boulder, beach, and sea in that order. On Burhou the cliffs are low and the descent is usually more of a scramble than a fall through space. The beam of our powerful torch showed that the puffling was safe in the water, and almost at once it dived.

At that moment a solitary Manx shearwater, passing over the dim sloe-black Swinge, gave out its wild crowing call. It was the first time I had heard this bird in the Channel Islands, where it does not breed, and it brought back to me memories of nights at Skokholm studying the fledgeling shearwaters. What a contrast these fledgeling puffins were! Through long practice of walking to and fro between nest and latrine within the burrow the young puffin, as we have seen, is quite nimble-footed. It may have exercised its wings often in the nest, but if so it must have found the burrow rather cramping. I must repeat that I have never seen the young puffin sitting outside its burrow like the young shearwater, which exercises its wings there night after night before finally taking to the sea. The explanation is simple: the shearwater at the burrow mouth is paying its first visit to the outside world; it has never before walked to its own front door, and it quite lacks the upright practised stance of the young puffin. Deserted by its parents the young shearwater is impelled at last to shuffle along the passage upon bent legs, until it reaches the exit; there it remains in a helpless attitude, beating its wings at the threshold for the first time in its life. It cannot

Simply everyone's favourite – the puffin.

75

walk properly, and at first it cannot fly; it can only shuffle over the ground, and it does not dare travel to the sea until it has spent several nights in stretching and exercising its wings on its front doorstep. Until it is ready to make the journey to the sea the lonely juvenile shearwater retires to the safety of the burrow before dawn – and the predatory gulls – surprise it.

Not so our deserted puffling. We have already described the bold exit, the impetuosity which makes it difficult to catch at the burrow entrance. Our torch may momentarily pick out the little white breast in its dazzling beam, and for the moment the bird is dazed enough for us, provided we keep the light steadily on it, to seize it in our hand. Often it walks away from the light, hurries away downhill, and flutters to the sea. For this reason – of a swift journey to the sea soon after nightfall – it is possible to surprise very few juveniles between the burrow exit and the water.

At 09.25 hours I entered the hide in order to film puffins. Here on Burhou the rogue gulls which were trying to snatch sand-eels and small fishes from the puffins were chiefly lesser black-backed gulls, of which there is a large colony on the island. One of these was studying the fish-carrying puffins, and making clumsy and unsuccessful rushes at them – it did not seem to be so expert as the rogue herring-gulls at Skokholm. Another was mauling the corpse of a puffling in the middle distance. It made three attempts to swallow it whole, while two adult puffins looked at it quizzically or turned to gaze the other way indifferently. Each time the gull failed it ejected the corpse, only to pick it up and try again, throat distended and head jerking viciously. After several failures it stood over the body and yodelled angrily. Once more it gulped and failed, choking down black bits of puffin fluff. At the next attempt it got the puffin's head down into its throat; violent jerks of the head and success seemed near. The meal was half swallowed, the legs and wings still showing, and the gull looked extremely uncomfortable. Moving a few paces away the gull stretched its neck and swallowed with brutish motions of the bursting gullet. Slowly the bill closed over the last leg and wing. The gull was now quite out of shape, the throat bulging in an ivory ball behind the head, which it turned this way and that in levering movements, and gradually screwed the monstrous meal towards the stomach. With all the appearance of acute indigestion the gull sat down on a little hillock with eyes half closed and neck and crown feathers puffed up like those of a sick bird.

Meanwhile the first gull had had some success with her piratical collisions with adult puffins, and was tenderly feeding her young chick on sand-eels and tiny fishes. She picked them up one by one from the ground and held them in her red-spotted yellow bill for the chick to nibble and devour, only swallowing those which were not accepted by her child. This appeared satisfied after it had taken four or five; the adult ate the rest and at once stalked on foot through the puffin assembly, making sallies at those near her arriving with fish.

Half an hour later the first gull walked down from the hillock of digestion and called. Two gull chicks advanced from hiding. The adult made retching motions and threw up the macerated fledgeling which it had swallowed with such difficulty. The chicks, as if protesting, called shrilly, but made no attempt to eat the horrid object on the ground. The adult, after staring at it herself (as if she wondered whether the effort were worth while), picked up the puffin and jerked it down her throat once more. It stuck half-way; and now the chicks eagerly attacked it, pulling at the legs and wings and torn body. I remembered that the young gull chicks respond to food only if it is held in the bill of the adult – on the ground it has almost no meaning for them until they are big or at least half grown. There is a bright red spot painted on the lower mandible of the adult, and this is said to guide the carnivorous baby gull, which stabs at it and thus comes into contact with the food held in the mouth of the adult. But these chicks could get little satisfaction out of pulling at the legs and wings of the puffling. They called shrilly and tugged unavailingly. Suddenly the parent, tired of this unprofitable struggle jerked the carcass down out of sight, and, marching back to the hillock, sat down uncomfortably. The chicks subsided in the spergularia. Evidently supper was not quite prepared yet!

Edmund Selous (*The Birdwatcher in the Shetlands*, 1905) was fascinated by the fishing and eating habits of the puffins themselves rather than their predators.

There is a puffin, now, within a few feet of me, with the largest fish I have yet seen one carrying; as large as a Cornish sardine, and that is as large as can possibly pass for one. And yet it has several smaller ones in its bill, besides. How is this done? For, to catch the big fish, it must have opened the beak a good deal. That one, however, is right at the base of the bill, as though it had been caught first. This, I think, supports my ideas as to the *modus operandi*. I do not see how so large a fish could be caught, without letting out any little ones that had gone before it. But if it were caught first, the beak, which can cut into the body, to the bird's convenience, need not be opened more widely, on the next occasion, than it would be if it held only a small fish. Did the big fish occupy any other position in the bill than that which it does, it would be against my theory; situated as it is, it is for it. Pray heaven, then, I don't see another puffin with a big fish! – for it may be held differently.

Yes, this is Tammy-Norie-land. Puffins are everywhere. They dot all the steep, green slopes, and cluster on the flat surfaces or salient angles of half the grey boulders that pierce the soil, or lie scattered all about it. Great crowds of them float on the sea, and other crowds oppress the air with constant, fastbeating pinions, passing continually from land to sea and from sea to land again, whilst many, on the latter journey, even though laden with fish, circle many times round, in a wide circumference, before finally settling. The soil, too, is honeycombed with their burrows, and in each of these, as well as in the nooks and chambers of rocks that lie closely together, there is a young fluffy black puffin, which increases the population by about a third, to say nothing of those parent birds which may also be underground. A million of puffins, I should think, must be standing, flying, or swimming in the more or less immediate vicinity; the air, especially, if it be a sunny day – or, rather, for a sunny minute or so – is like one great sunbeam full of little dancing bird-motes. On the shore they stand together in friendly groups and clusters, and leave it for those much larger gatherings where they ride, hundreds together, ducking and bobbing on the light waves like a fleet of little painted boats, each one with a highly ornamental bird or, rather, puffin-headed prow. Thus their duties are carried on under the mantle of social pleasure; it is all a coming and going between a land-party and a sea-party, so that the domestic life of these birds would be a type and pattern of feminine happiness if only they were a little – by which I mean vastly – more noisy. Puffins indeed are somewhat silent birds – at least they have been so during the time I have seen them – from the middle of June, that is to say, till the middle of August – though as they can and do utter with effect, on occasions, they are, perhaps, more vociferous at an earlier period, before domestic matters have become so far advanced. Not that amidst such a huge number of them, their note – which I have described – is not frequently heard; but still, whatever I have seen them doing they have generally been doing it dumbly. This includes the series of funny little bows or bobs, accompanied by a shuffling from one foot to the other, which the male, one may say with certainty, is in the habit of making to the female, but which probably the female – as in the case of other sea-birds

I have mentioned – also sometimes makes to the male. A display of this sort is usually followed by a little kissing or nebbing match, after which, one of the birds, standing so as directly to face the other, will often raise, and then again lower, the head, some eight or nine times in succession, in a half solemn manner, at the same time opening its gaudy beak, sometimes to a considerable extent, yet all the while without uttering a sound. All this looks very affectionate, but I have often remarked that after one such display and interchange of endearments, the bird that has initiated or taken the leading part in both, turns to another, and repeats, or offers to repeat, the performance – for on such occasions it does not, as a rule, receive much encouragement from the second bird.

Hardly any bird has a more perfect shape than an Arctic skua. Let us watch them with Selous (*The Birdwatcher in the Shetlands*, 1905).

These Arctic skuas bathe together very prettily. They sit high and light on the water, duck their heads under it, and throw it over them with

The Arctic skua has one of the most perfect shapes of any seabird.

79

their wings. Between their ablutions they often sport in the air, swooping at and chasing one another. Their motions are such as one might imagine those of elemental spirits to be, and their wild cry adds to this imaginary resemblance. Oh, that cry, that wild, wild cry, that music of the winds, the clouds, the drifting rain and mist – like them, free as them, voicing their freedom, making their spirit articulate! Who can describe it, or put down into poor, paltry syllables the glory that lives in it? Let none try. Let no clumsy imitation disfigure it, but let it live for ever in the memory of him who has sat on the great ness-side, on the dividing-line of sea and sky, and heard it pealing so clearly, so cheerly, so gladly wild, so wildly, madly glad. So let it come to him again in his own soul's music, scudding with the clouds, driving with the driving mists, ringing out like "the wild bells to the wild sky." And never let that sky be blue that it rings to, unless in pale, moist patches, drowning amidst watery clouds; and never let there be a sun, to be called one, but only a glint and a gleaming, a storming of stormy light, a wet beam flung on a rain-cloud. Child of the mists, of the grey-eyed and desolate north-land, what hast thou to do with the robes of the vine and the olive? To be brief, I know of no cry, of no voice so exhilarating as that of this poetic bird.

Seton Gordon's book *In Search of Northern Birds* (1941) contains a passage about great skuas, for which he also uses the local name 'bonxie'.

The voyager from Aberdeen or Leith to the Shetland Islands perhaps notices, while yet that island group is invisible, that a strange bird joins the seagulls following the steamer. The newcomer is a large, dark brown bird, with an area of white on either wing, and its flight is undistinguished, and apparently aimless, until a seagull swoops down and picks up a scrap of meat which has been dropped overboard by the cook. The great skua – for this is the name of the dark brown bird – which has been idly following the ship then shoots forward, like a racing car which is suddenly accelerated by its driver, overtakes the gull, and very soon forces it to drop or disgorge its prize.

There is something remarkable in the sudden speeding-up of the great skua's flight and the impression is given of most formidable power in reserve. The great skua, or bonxie, as it is almost universally named in Shetland, is so powerful that even the greater black-backed gull is afraid of it. A light-keeper of the Out Skerries light told me that he watched one day a bonxie deliberately murdering a greater black back on the rocks below the lighthouse, and I heard of a great skua which, on seeing a greater black-backed gull snatch a herring from the deck of a drifter in Lerwick Sound, swooped down, killed the great gull with a single blow, swallowed the herring, then flew unperturbed away, as though slaying greater black backs was an everyday affair.

On the water below the great cliffs of Noss I saw another bird tragedy. East of Lerwick, chief port of Shetland, is Bressay Isle, and east of Bressay is the grassy isle of Noss, inhabited only by a shepherd. On its east face Noss is a sheer precipice, and the cliffs, 600 feet high, appear even higher when viewed from the sea immediately below them.

It was on a July morning that my friend and I left Lerwick in a small open motor boat, and passed out through the Sound to the open sea to the north. In Lerwick harbour the scene was an animated one. Hundreds of herring drifters were moored to the quays, and to one another. Boats from Yarmouth and Lowestoft rubbed shoulders with Scottish craft from Peterhead, Fraserburgh and ports of the Moray Firth. Out in the Sound were anchored fishing craft from Holland and Norway, and there were fish-carriers from Germany and the Balkan States. At intervals, between misty showers, the sky over the sea was a deep blue.

We steered north through the entrance to the Sound, where many fulmars were resting on the deep blue water or flying gracefully above the sea, and felt the lift of the north-easterly swell which broke white against Beosetter Holm and Score Head. Soon we had left Bressay astern and were sailing along the north coast of Noss. As we approached the great cliffs on the east side of that island we saw many birds ahead of us, and it was here that I realized first the reprehensible habits of the bonxie, which has increased so greatly that it has now been removed from the list of protected birds in certain districts of Shetland.

On the sea beneath the great precipice of Noss a bonxie was deliberately murdering a kittiwake. Like a winged stoat, the great skua had attached itself to the victim's back and was eating away the flesh at the back of the neck while the kittiwake flapped its wings despairingly, and attempted to rise from the water and throw off the deadly grip of its implacable enemy. We rescued the kittiwake, but too late to save its life.

In *Pirates and Predators* (1959), Colonel Richard Meinertzhagen describes his own, and some second-hand, experiences of the hunting habits of great skuas.

At Hoy in Orkney in 1938 there were twenty-four pair of great skua

The great skua is big and heavy – but has a good turn of speed.

breeding, their main food being kittiwake and puffin; we found the remains of many dozen of these birds and we estimated that about fifty victims must be secured every day. The skuas would lie in wait for the puffins returning to their burrows, quickly assault them, knock them on the head and at once commence to eat the breast. Often the puffin, laden with fish, would slip into his hole before the skua could catch him. But the skua knew his job and would wait just above the hole and knock the wretched puffin out as he emerged. We noticed at Hoy that ravens give the skua a wide berth but peregrines and harriers usually ignore them, though the latter is attacked if it approaches the nest. We never saw a skua molest a fulmar at Hoy, though the latter was abundant.

In Shetland this skua is abundant. In August I witnessed a remarkable combined operation against an eider and her brood by this skua and a great northern diver. The eider had three very small ducklings. The skua would swoop down, compelling them to dive, whilst the diver would submerge and, catching them under water, would surface and swallow them. In the end, the skua secured one duckling while the diver secured another. The third duckling disappeared and must have been secured by either the skua or the diver. The skua sat on the water to eat his duckling.

A. Hazelwood (personal communication) records that in autumn the great skua when attacking eider utters a loud call which attracts kittiwake who later partake of the feast when the skua has finished.

The local crofters begged us to shoot all the skuas as they had lost seven lambs from attacks in one spring. Also in Shetland we noticed that small colonies of terns were powerless to resist an attack by skuas and in every small colony not a single chick got off, but in the larger colonies combined action by the terns would beat off an attack.

One of the victims of the skuas' attacks, the kittiwake, is a member of the gull family – birds which are easily dismissed as somehow unworthy of attention. Yet they are extraordinarily beautiful, as Fisher and Lockley remind us in *Seabirds* (1954).

Gulls are strong aggressive well-built birds with long wings capable of sustained and powerful flight. They have webbed feet, but are good walkers on land. In the air they move with ease and grace, and glide without effort for long distances. The majority have white bodies with grey or black mantles or wings. Some have a dark hood during the breeding season, but this is moulted in the autumn. The young gulls are more difficult to identify in the field, the juvenile and first year plumages of the larger species being a drab mottled brown.

The full beauty of flight of the gulls may be watched from the deck of a ship, when it will be seen that gulls are expert at taking advantage of the wind-eddies caused by the passage of the vessel; again and again they skim and circle about the ship, using the wind deflected against the hull to lift them, with scarcely any movement of their outspread wings. Over land they frequently soar, wheeling upon a thermal pocket of air and spiralling to a great height with no more than an occasional beat of the wings and twist of the tail. On the water they swim buoyantly as they scavenge for food. They are however poor divers and rarely submerge completely.

Kenneth Williamson studied kittiwakes in the Faeroes, and in particular the village of Mykines. In *The Atlantic Islands* (1948), he relates his findings.

The prating of the stream to its narrow stony bed and the clamour of the sharp-tongued kittiwakes make a constant musical background to the Mykines life and scene. The village has character from this endless argument of the crowds of white birds nesting so close at hand, for, even though they are for the most part out of sight, they are never beyond hearing. You wake in the morning to this babel of tongues; you walk and work and eat with it as a perpetual accompaniment, and when you go to bed it is still singing in your ears. Throughout the half-darkness that passes in the Faeroe summer for dead of night it is the stuff of the village silence. For silence exists in the familiar sounds you do not consciously hear rather than in no sound at all, and if you take the silence of Mykines apart it resolves itself into these components, the garrulity of the little stream and the highpitched voices of the innumerable gulls. They create a kind, comforting, friendly silence, for after the first few hours you cease to think of it as noise. Perhaps the Mykines men, despite their playful remark that "*Rita* will stop crying before women stop talking!" are not really aware of it at all – until they realise with sorrow in September that the sound has stopped, the kittiwakes have left, and the long and stormy winter is at hand.

To look at, kittiwakes are the daintiest of the commoner gulls, but it is a great pity that their domestic habits do not match their appearance.

Of all the gulls, the kittiwake is perhaps the most delicate.

Small, trim and immaculate, they are a joy to watch on the wing, and when looking down from their nests on the cliff-face, with heads inclined to one side, they have a demure expression that is quite remarkable in a gull. But they have astonishingly filthy habits, and if you want to find abject squalor in the bird-world the kittiwake colony is the place to look for it. It is anomalous that such a pretty creature is not more fastidious in its home-life – just as it is that the kingfisher, sparkling gem of English waterways, lives in a nesting-tunnel like an open drain. Because their persons are so pleasing one is disappointed that their habits are not equally above reproach.

When new the kittiwake's nest is a wonder of skill and tidiness: a compact cushion of grass and seaweed, it is placed – almost glued – against the cliff-face on any slight projection big enough to support its base. For economy of living-space reduced to a fine art there is nothing in nature to compare with a crowded kittiwake tenement. Now, however, at the end of the season, the nests were chalked and filthy with fishy offal and the birds' own droppings, and they reeked offensively in the summer sun. Not only were the nests themselves badly fouled, but the cliff was everywhere splodged with white patches, or held small gutters and channels in which fish-castings and droppings blended together in a noisome, fly-delighting mess. There were times when climbing was difficult because the rocks were slippery with this semi-liquid ooze, or was impossible because the only available handhold had been anointed by innumerable birds in the most disgusting fashion!

Kittiwakes are vulnerable to larger gulls, as well as skuas, as a passage from Edmund Selous' *The Birdwatcher in the Shetlands* (1905) demonstrates.

All doubt as to the real nature of these horrid feastings of the herring-gulls on floating carcases of kittiwakes is now at an end. I had been watching the seals in one pool, when, turning to the other, I saw, as I thought, two gulls fighting together on one of the great rocks in the midst of it – a smaller "stack" one might almost call it. Raising the glasses, the truth was revealed. It was a herring-gull murdering a young kittiwake, and very soon it would have been "got done" – as Carlyle says with such a gusto – if I had not, in rising to follow it more closely, alarmed the murderer, who at once flew away. The poor little kittiwake got up – for it had been thrown on its back – and stood without moving on the rock, presenting a sick and sorry appearance, though there was as yet no blood about it, and it did not appear to have been seriously hurt.

Its only chance now was to have flown away, but it stayed and stayed, seeming to doze after a while – the certain victim of the returning gull, as soon as the latter should have watched me off.

Turning my eyes from this disquieting spectacle – one brick in God's architecture – I looked over the water, and there, in this quiet little bay, which seems such a haven of rest and peace – *il mio retiro,* one would think, to every creature in it – I saw another kittiwake being savagely murdered by another herring-gull. This was a repulsive sight, and through the glasses I could watch it closely, not a detail escaping. The gull, with the hook of its bill fixed in the kittiwake's throat, pressed it down on the water, shook it with violence, paused, got a better purchase, shook it again, then, opening and gobbling up with the mandibles, seemed to be trying to crush the head, or compress the throat, between them. By this the young bird's struggles, which had been of an innocent and quite ineffectual kind, had almost ceased, but its legs still kicked in the air as it lay on its back in the water – just as the other had lain on the rock. The gull now, having managed the preliminaries, ceased to be so rough and violent, but, backing a little out from the body, so as to get the proper swing, began, in a cold, deliberate manner, to pickaxe down into the exposed breast, each blow ending in a bite and tear. A crimson spot, becoming gradually larger and larger till it represented almost the whole upper surface, as the body cavity was laid open, responded to this treatment; and now the gull, seizing upon entrail and organ, helped each backward pull with a flap or two of the wings, feasting redly and royally.

So it goes on, and, in time, both the part-players in this little sample fragment of an infinitely great whole are drifted by the waves to that same towering "stack" which has lately been the scene of the puffin tragedy. On it the gull lands, and, having dragged the carcase some way up, flings his head into the air, and exults with a wild, vociferous cry, in which his mate, who has now joined him, takes part. Then there is more feasting; but in spite of the community of feeling which this duet implies, the second gull is not allowed to partake of the good cheer, but must wait till the provider of it has finished. Should she approach too near, such intrusion is vigorously repelled. Well, thank God for the touch of poetry, whenever it appears! There is something picturesquely wild, as well as savage, in the latter part of this sea-scene – the gull's *te deum,* flung out to sea and sky; but anything more horrid, more ignobly, sordidly vile than what has preceded it, it would be hard to imagine. A kittiwake in its first full plumage, which differs much from the parents', is a very pretty bird, dove-like and innocent-looking. To see it savagely

The herring gull is a successful, adaptable bird, at home almost anywhere.

shaken and flung about, a huge hooked implement fastened in its slender throat, and that soft little head towzled, bitten on, mumbled, the wings all the while flapping in helpless and quite futile efforts to escape, is sickening. It is not the worst scene in nature certainly – serious deliberation amongst enlightened statesmen can produce things a good deal more horrible – but it is bad enough, bad enough. It looks like the negation of God, but a much better case can be made out for its being the affirmation, so here is the consolatory reflection for which optimists are never at a loss. "There's comfort yet," as Macbeth says.

Finally, let G. and A. Marples, from their book *Sea Terns or Sea Swallows* (1934), describe some of the fascination of this super-elegant, yet bold and aggressive, group.

At no time does a ternery seem anything less than beautiful. Crowded with birds in Summer or when left untenanted in Winter; under every condition of weather; at dawn; throughout the day; as night falls; even during the night itself, the ternery is full of charm. What forms the particular attraction is not easy to determine, though it would seem to be bound up in the word "grey," for not even the most vivid sunshine can eliminate the greyness which is inherent in everything which goes to make up the atmosphere and environment of the Terns. But to say this does not mean that a ternery is colourless; on the contrary, it is full of colour, not obvious hues, but those indeterminate and of the most subtle tenderness.

Through the night all is vague-colour and form. One senses the shapes of the surrounding sandhills which cannot be seen; they are no more than a slightly more opaque form of the luminous greyness which envelops everything. The soft darkness not only obscures the reality of things, it muffles the swish of wind-stirred marram grass; it dulls the roar of the distant waters, still uneasy after yesterday's storm. It is 3 a.m. when, from the east, comes an intangible change. The settled silence which has aided the darkness in its effort to hide the birds is disturbed by a general uneasiness, felt rather than heard – the first sign of awakening. Whether the birds see or feel the dawn-change which can hardly be described as light, it has an immediate effect. Then a Lark is heard high above, singing in the still dark sky, and at once, all around, many others burst into a full-throated chorus. None can be seen. Now a faint light develops eastwardly, slowly evolving into a narrow band of greenish-yellow. As gradually a long, low line of cloud is disclosed crossing the sky, overtopped by a grey range slightly warmer in colour. Where unclouded, the sky is a cold grey-blue. The sandhills materialise as warm black silhouettes against the dawn. The wakened Terns are now heard calling all around; cries arrive from those already in amorous flight in the upper air, and from those still on the ground comes a continuous, grating clamour. Flitting through the dim dawn-light, appear and fade nebulous ghostly forms, pale against the still dark sky and darker sandhills. Some call suddenly and harshly as they pass; most are silent. The light strengthens as the dim yellow bar creeps slowly upwards. The warm clouds assume a rusty hue, nothing dramatic, menacing only, as the wind increases and with fitful gusts tugs at the tent in which we are hiding. The dim, grey forms surrounding us are now seen to be sitting Terns, trembling with eagerness as they nestle closer on their eggs. A silence descends on the scene. The Lark's chorus is ended. The sky is empty of the beating, flying Terns. All except the sitting birds have gone off to the fishing, to the cold, grey sea lying over there. Soon one and another are seen returning, some with a tiny fish hanging from their beak. All are uttering cheerful cries. With a burst of light comes the full day; the business of life has commenced.

A blazing setting sun is reflected as molten silver in the wet bay behind the sandhills. As it drops, the silver changes to a burning glow on either side of which the shallow water, overspreading the flat muddy sand, gleams gold and pink and milky opal. A flock of Dunlins, black against the shining sea, arrive on gliding wings and alight on the edge of the water. The uncovered area of the flat, like the sandhills in the ternery, is cold heavy grey, in violent contrast with the delicately rippled opal water. A few Terns are still love-making in the air, the rest having alighted on the beach to roost. The shallow, advancing tide runs over the flat, swinging round to the right in a delicious curve, blue-grey

The Arctic tern is one of the greatest travellers in the world.

in hue, edged with golden pearl. Following the moving water, thigh deep, and busily feeding, come the Dunlins. The tiny waves break with a gentle "plop," a crash in miniature. Now dark grey-green yet glittering golden, they run up the shore like gliding, living things, sinuous sea-beasts, parabolically curved. Beyond and among them the surface is golden-opal laced with lilac-grey and rippled with milky-blue. Chill and forbidding heave the shoulders of the cold, heavy grey ternery dunes, softened on their edges by the dull, hueless, waving grass. Afar off, sandbanks fringed on the seaward edge with pale grey breakers form a warm band of colour crossing the cool grey of the heaving sea. As we watch, four seals appear; one drags himself laboriously upon the sand, leaving its mates to frisk and gambol in the near-by water. Soon they too will emerge and creep heavily up the bank, writhing like dark brown slugs. Perhaps they will be joined by others to the number of twenty-eight as they were the other day. With the fading of the light, the brilliance of the water in the bay departs, leaving an expanse of cold hueless grey, rather lighter than the hills. No bird life is now to be seen. The Dunlins have flown. The Terns have settled for the night and are invisible, enveloped in the on-creeping gloom. All save one pair high in the sky but unseen, report of whose whereabouts comes to us through their reiterated calls. Soon these aerial cries cease, the birds have dropped swiftly to the beach to join their roosting friends, and as the last, tenuous light fades from the west, the night-quiet settles over the ternery for the hours of darkness.

Seabirds have inspired many a birdwatcher and writer about birds. Perhaps more than any other group they are at one with their world – wild, powerful ocean and raw coastline which can be so serene, so calm and beautiful one day and so viciously torn by wind and waves the next. They allow escapism in birdwatching to a greater degree than almost anything else. They are perhaps nearest to being unaffected by man, at least upon superficial examination, and something to be especially treasured.

3 BIRDS OF PREY

Birds of prey have had a special fascination for many people, in many different cultures and civilisations, for thousands of years. In modern Europe, most species are greatly reduced and restricted in range but there are still wilderness areas where many may be found. These are birds which hunt and kill other birds and animals for food, or which eat animals found already dead. Many are large, striking and impressive, often flying with incomparable ability; some are very rare and found in wild, remote countryside. So they evoke a wide range of responses (good and bad) and have received more than their fair share of attention in the literature.

In *Pirates and Predators* (1959), Colonel Richard Meinertzhagen defended the raptors.

Birds and beasts of prey do not hunt for sport except in very rare cases: a fox killing a pheasant is going about his lawful business; an eagle taking a grouse is doing so to enable him to exist. The larger cats and all hawks kill in a more humane fashion than does man. There is very little wounding, and death is usually instantaneous.

Man's desire to kill predatory animals probably survives from the days when he had to compete with cave bears and sabre-toothed tigers and when gangs of hairy Neanderthalers would mob the lion with the same noise and fuss which accompany the mobbing of an owl by tits and thrushes today, except that Neanderthal man probably threw stones and logs of wood. Today it is seldom that a gamekeeper can resist shooting any hawk or owl he sees – the larger and more unusual the bird, the more readily will he shoot. That type of man probably constitutes the greatest danger and does the greatest harm to many forms of wild life; and the sportsman with the gamekeeper's mentality is little better – possibly worse – for he should know better. The excuse is that objectionable word "vermin". Every conceivable form of wild life which might possibly disturb game is classed as vermin, whereas the most dangerous disturber of wild life and the greatest vermin of all is man himself. The sportsman, the egg-collector, the bird-lover, bird-photographer and bird-watcher are all greater disturbers and destroyers of wild life than any wild predator, who after all is going about his lawful business – survival. I am not preaching anti-bloodsport propaganda and I recognise man's right to kill for food, for science, or to protect his own property; but he has no right to kill for the love of killing or endeavour to exterminate animals whose lawful pursuit is killing for food.

Some of Meinertzhagen's views could still be aired with profit today.

Magpies and jays, two of the most attractive and beautiful birds of the countryside, are ruthlessly persecuted and shot by gamekeepers and sportsmen with the mentalities of keepers; the harm they do to game birds is negligible; the pleasure they give to the public is immense. Moreover, I know of estates where both jays and magpies abound alongside an abundance of not only game but other small birds. To destroy these birds in order to give pleasure to men who enjoy killing other birds is morally wrong and cannot be justified.

If I may add a personal note, it would be for full protection for the jay.

Many of the current threats to raptors are not new. In 1913 Francis Heatherley wrote a book about peregrines (*The Peregrine Falcon at the Eyrie*); this was the dedication:

To all egg collectors in the hope that some day they will realise that the shell is not the most important part of a bird's egg.

Some of the earlier problems and charges levelled against the raptors have nevertheless disappeared. William Macgillivray, in *Rapacious Birds of Great Britain* (1836), recounts some early stories about white-tailed eagles.

In almost every district in the Highlands stories are told of eagles that have carried away infants temporarily left by their mothers in the harvest field or elsewhere; and it is probable that such an occurrence may have taken place, although the evidence is usually imperfect. Sir Robert

White-tailed eagles are the subject of a reintroduction scheme in the Hebrides.

Sibbald states, that in Orkney "an eagle seized a child, a year old, which its mother had left, wrapped up in some clothes, at a place called Houton-Head, while she went for a few moments to gather sticks for firewood, and carried it a distance of four miles to Hoia; which circumstance being known from the cries of the mother, four men went there in a boat, and, knowing where the nest was, found the child unhurt and untouched."

Of the many absurd stories told of eagles, the following, by the justly celebrated geologist Von Buch, is not the least remarkable. "We learned," says he, "with astonishment, that eagles were very much dreaded on these islands; for they are not contented with lambs and smaller animals, but even attack oxen, and not unfrequently master them. The manner of their attack is so singular that we should have doubted the truth of the account if we had not heard it so circumstantially and distinctly confirmed to us, in the same terms, at places a great distance from each other. The eagle plunges itself into the waves, and after being completely drenched, rolls itself among the sand on the shore till its wings are quite covered with sand. It then rises into the air, and hovers over its unfortunate victim. When it is close to it, it shakes its wings, and throws stones and sand into the eyes of the ox, and completes the terror of the animal by blows with its powerful wings. The blinded oxen run about quite raving, and at length fall down completely exhausted, or dash themselves to death from some cliff. The eagle then mangles, undisturbed, the fruits of its victory." If this tale be true, the Norwegian eagles must be very different from ours in courage and sagacity; for the British eagles, in so far as I have seen, are so cowardly that they do not even venture to defend their nests against a solitary rocksman, dangling upon a rope like a spider upon a thread, and so weak, or rather so unable to rise with speed, that they seldom attempt to carry off a lamb unless in windy weather, and from an eminence. But as to eagles plunging into the waves with the view of getting drenched, in order that sand might adhere to their draggled plumes, and then flying off to blind oxen with it, – this requires to be established by respectable witnesses before it can be credited.

In *Pirates and Predators* (1959), Meinertzhagen also described the trapping of white-tailed, or sea, eagles.

Eagle-trapping was for time out of mind a regular occupation on Vaeröy and Röst, and only when head-money could no longer be claimed for the birds did the practice finally die out. Thome, the Norwegian ornithologist, has left some interesting notes on the simple, almost primitive stratagem employed. Hard by some eagle-haunted fell the trapper dug a pit about a yard deep, around which he built a rough stone hut of equal height, finally adding a roof of stone slabs. The entrance he closed with a large piece of turf. A little distance away was displayed some carrion, usually a sheep's entrails, secured by a cord which led into the hut. On a favourable morning the trapper would begin his patient vigil before daylight. Sometimes he had not long to wait before an eagle appeared. Even when most sharp-set, the bird would always break off its gorging at intervals to look around for possible dangers. Whenever it was so employed, the trapper carefully drew the carrion a little nearer to the hut. So far from showing any uneasiness as the lure moved, the eagle would tear at it the more fiercely. If all went well, the bird would follow its meal right up to the hut, when the trapper, waiting until his quarry's attention was once more distracted, would seize it by the legs and drag it in. Finding itself in the utter darkness behind the turf curtain, the eagle would offer no resistance. If two or more eagles were at the bait together, it sometimes happened that when the first was captured the others continued feeding. With luck, a trapper could catch two or three eagles in a few hours. But his patience often went unrewarded, and there he would remain crouched in the hut until darkness fell. The trappers worked from the end of October until Christmas, the season's catch varying between fifty and a hundred. In the 'eighties and 'nineties an eagle was worth three kroner to its captor, who claimed two-thirds of the sum as head-money, and earned the remainder by selling the wings to be used as brooms.

Leslie Brown, in his book called *Eagles*, published in 1955, described the way in which these awesome birds have captured and held man's attention over the centuries.

The eagle is one of those few birds which for ever hold a fascination for mankind. From the Bible times, when the way of an eagle in the air was classed as equally wonderful with the way of a serpent on the earth and the way of a man with a maid, through a long series of fable and legend, down to modern times when authors have written more books about eagles than about any other sort of bird, except possibly some seabirds, the fascination has been undimmed. Eagles stand in impossible attitudes on so many gateposts, appear on so many heraldic bearings, and, nowadays, excite so much attention in the popular press and give their names to so many advertisements, magazines, and even motor tyres, that it is clear that through the ages the eagle has ever been to man a strange and wonderful creature, classed with the lion and the unicorn, the gryphon and the dragon.

Nor is it difficult, really, to see why. The way of an eagle in the air is as remarkable today as ever it was, and no one who has seen the perfect grace and control, the effortless ease, of an eagle soaring over wild country – and who has a mind to look at it – can fail to be impressed. The eagle threads the paths of the upper air in a manner eclipsed by no other bird; vultures, storks and pelicans may soar efficiently and even grandly, but they cannot – or do not – match the agility of an eagle as he makes his stoop upon his prey. The peregrine, or any other large falcon, can pester an eagle many times his size, and lovers of the falcon will often say that the eagle flees in terror. Totally untrue if they do; the eagle merely takes himself off from a tiresome presence, and will, occasionally, turn over in exasperation and present his claws to the pesterer, who knows well that if they were to clutch it would be the end of him. The instant alarm of lower creatures at the sight of an eagle, the grouse pack fleeing on the Scottish tops, the gazelle suddenly crouching on the plains, the monkey barking from the shelter of a tree, all testify to his strength and power. He is the king of birds, he has no regular enemies in the natural order of things, other than man. He is the avian counterpart of the lion, the tiger, and the elephant, and like those greater creatures, he must in the end die an ignoble death of starvation or old age. This is the inevitable penalty of being at the top of the tree.

It was many years ago that I had my first meeting with an eagle. It was in a hot Indian compound, and I was watching with interest some Egyptian Vultures and kites disputing refuse under a large banyan tree. Quite suddenly, another bird arrived among them. Brown, like a kite, but larger, and with his powerful legs feathered to the toes – the hallmark of all the true eagles – he stalked forward. The kites and vultures drew back. The Tawny Eagle, for such he was, tramped steadily up to whatever they had been eating, took what he wanted, and withdrew to a tree-top where he consumed it at leisure. The kites and vultures returned, but superiority had been proclaimed.

Many years later, upon the Scottish hills, I studied the Golden Eagle with a fervour and energy given to few. I traversed endless miles of hill in good weather and bad, and was rewarded now and again by glimpses of the eagle which live for ever in the mind. A small speck, poised effortlessly in a blue sky above the snow cornices of a remote corrie where I lay in the sun; a great dark bird, suddenly met in the mist as he swept over the summit of a mountain in the Monadhliaths, and looked for a startled second into my eyes as he passed; a soaring eagle, quartering the flanks of Ben a Chlachair, some hundreds of feet below me and unaware of my presence, his wing-tips delicately playing with the light airs of a hot summer's day; an eagle plunging at speed a thousand feet downward, turning up above the burn in the bottom of the glen, and coming to rest on the nest his mate had just left, after a curving swoop of such perfect timing that he had only to close his wings entirely at the appropriate moment to come to a stop – poetry of motion indeed. Such memories will crowd upon anyone who has watched eagles upon the hills, and at each fresh manifestation I feel a rush of pleasure. The eagle is now a familiar being to me, but I still see things from time to time that I never dreamt of, and there will always be mystery and unknown regions to explore.

There is another side to it, and perhaps a greater. Watching eagles entails many thousands of miles of tramping in the waste and wild places of the earth. This is no easy bird to know; he does not come to any bird table. There may be, and still are, places where eagles are relatively common; I have found some of them myself. But mostly, eagles live in small numbers in wild mountainous regions or large areas of uninhabited bush or desert, sea cliffs or other places of the sort away from the fringes of man's existence. Every sport or amusement has its ancillary pleasures; the fisherman is a poor sort who cannot enjoy the day by the stream even when he catches no fish; the exhilaration of a rock climb will be balanced by the feeling of well-being when one lies on the turf at the top and admires the view. So it is with eagles; you go out to look for them, and in the process you come to many strange and wonderful places. It may be the richly aromatic floor of a pine forest in Speyside, where you can idle away an hour or two and watch the ants and the Crested Tits – and eat blaeberries betimes. It may be a high corniced ridge on a perfect early spring day, when the sky is blue and clear, dappled with clouds, and the wind throws spicules of snow above your head as you walk along in shelter, feeling a surge of well-being in the wine-like air. Or it may be a stark crag rearing holdless from an endless sea of thornbush, where just back from the lip of the precipice, you can sit in the shade of a forest tree and look outwards over the illimitable space of Africa, over a red parched plain to distant blue ranges, regaled by the sweet whistling of Red-winged Starlings and the effortless manoeuvre of the eagles, ravens, hawks, and swifts that circle about the face of this remote mountain. All such places are wonderful, and they are not reached without some tribulation; they are the other half of eagle hunting. You may see no eagles, or, when you become a connoisseur, you may not find the particular eagle you seek, but these other sights and sounds will compensate, as they do in many another pursuit. In time they may become the more important of the two; the eagle may be subordinated to his surroundings.

The surroundings of the sought-after eagle may become equal to, or even greater than, the bird itself in the appeal and overall experience for some people. Seton Gordon, in many books, here illustrated from *Days with the Golden Eagle* (1927), surely evoked the quality of the bird's surroundings better than most.

Although winter still lingered in this upland glen the grouse were pairing, so that there was much animation among the "heather cocks" this morning and rivalry over the claiming of nesting territory. For some time two old cock grouse flew excitedly backwards and forwards, the pursuer never allowing the pursued to rest until they both alighted for breath upon the short heather.

In February a fierce southerly gale had swept the glen. It had piled the soft powdery snows high in sheltered hollows, and in one place the track was buried beneath fully 20 feet of snow, so firmly packed that one could walk on its surface without sinking in an inch.

At the head of the glen is the lonely hill loch. From it the cliffs rise sheer to a height of almost 4000 feet, and in these black rocks the golden eagle has her eyrie. I knew the eagle was at home to-day because of the behaviour of the grouse. They flew high overhead, moving this way and that, and seeming very unsettled and worried. Soon the eagle flew silently past, following closely the contour of the hill and sailing only a few feet above the ground. The great feather-clad legs were held outstretched towards the ground, in order, no doubt, that the eagle might grasp the more readily any luckless grouse or hare that might suddenly come in the field of her keen vision. I passed beneath the eyrie, but as yet there was no sign that the eagle had commenced to repair her home.

The hill loch to-day resembled some sheet of water of the Arctic. At the north end of the loch, where the waters are shallow, much ice was stranded. Here and there from the frozen shallows large rounded heaps of ice rose. They were shaped like ant-hills, and were of unusual and arresting appearance. They had apparently been formed by the showers of spray which a southerly gale had continuously thrown over some stranded ice-floes. Immediately it touched them the spray had frozen, so that an ever-thickening icy covering had grown up around the floes.

Along the margin of the loch I made my way. Near the farther shore a goosander drake drifted like a small iceberg upon the water. Deep, unbroken snow extended to the water's edge. The wild sheep which have now lived on these hills for a decade (they escaped being "gathered" when the hills were under sheep during the years of the

War) were tamed by hunger. They had been scraping for food near the water, and it was a tribute to their vigour that they had survived the snowfall which had covered the hills for a full eight weeks.

In the corrie above the loch a couple of cock ptarmigan were pursuing each other on snowy wings, for even thus high spring was stirring the pulses of living things. But soon the sun was obscured, and from the north a menacing squall of snow drifted quickly up the glen and soon reached the loch. Before its coming the air had been calm and the loch unruffled, but as the squall reached the loch a dark line showed on the margin of the hill waters as the icy wind current stirred them. Swiftly the breeze passed along the loch, and from the grim precipices the snow was caught up in powdery clouds that seemed black against the darkening skyline high above the loch. Across the cliffs the Polar wind made stern music; the corries were hidden in drifting snow. Soon the farther shore of the loch was invisible, and the snow and hail, scarcely melting in the icy water, floated on the surface in long grey lines as though they were foam whipped up by the wind.

Against the ice-barrier, which projected almost everywhere from the snowy slopes a few yards into the water, the spray from momentarily increasing waves spouted high. Ever more fiercely did the wind blow, and in the gathering gloom the grey snow was drifted past in ghostly clouds.

When, for a minute, the storm lessened I saw the eagle perched upon the hill-top opposite. On a knife-like ridge the great bird stood, seemingly indifferent to the bitter wind, then, as I watched, she (it was the hen bird) sprang magnificently into space and mounted on her broad wings on the frosty breeze. Always upon that narrow aerial ridge the eagle stands: in winter when all the hills sleep below their soft covering of snow; in summer when at noon the deer in the grassy corrie below drowse in the warm stillness. Here, from her lofty perch, the eagle can see hill, loch, and corrie, and westward, peak upon peak merging, in the far, dream-like distance, in the last mountain outposts that guard the approaches to Tir nan Og. Does her mind ponder upon those vast distances, great even for her with her unrivalled flight? Or does she watch rather for the swift-wheeling ptarmigan that drift in a white-winged clan across the loch far below; or the mountain hares that play upon the hill-face where the heather is not too long; or perhaps the golden plover that speed past on arrow-swift flight calling for the things that have gone away upon the breeze of the hills and will return no more?

But there is one object that her keen eye is ever eager to see, and that is the dark form of her mate – for the golden eagle pairs for life, and is as constant in her affections as she is stern and bold in her nature. How wonderful it is when her mate appears to see the two mount up on dark pinions! Up, and ever up, the two rise, sailing together far above the topmost peaks and entering the country of the winds and the soft, drifting clouds, where they fly at such an immense height that they are invisible to the eye.

An encounter with a golden eagle can be very short, despite hours of anticipation; but it may leave a lasting impression. Kenneth Richmond described it well in *Wild Venture* (1958).

So brief, so abrupt is the encounter that you are left with a sense of anti-climax when it is over. It is the kind of incident which only the cine-camera can record successfully – only who would be fiddling around with a cine-camera, all thumbs at the critical moment and so missing the whole thing? Still, it has to be admitted that human eyes are a shade too slow to make the most of their chances on such high occasions. As with all triumphs that are hard come by, whether it is winning the Derby or setting foot on the summit of Everest, the big moment is here and gone before you can seize hold of it. And yet, looking back, there is a once-and-for-all quality about it which stamps it into your very being: for the rest of your days will never forget this scene and all its details – the blue shadows of the clouds trailing up the farther slopes, the pincushions of moss campion, pinks on the rock-face, the clump of rose-root sprouting below the nest, the hollow voice of the Cuckoo below in the glen . . . And to think that all the time you were plodding up here – for two long hours – you were being kept under observation by both cock and hen Eagle, and that neither gave the game away until the very last moment. No wonder some eyries are hard to find.

Henry Seebohm knew eagles and their haunts well. In *A History of British Birds* (1885), he wrote the following.

The flight of the Golden Eagle is truly a grand performance. Stroll up the mountain-side some bright May morning when there is but little wind and the sun is warm, and see the bird engaged in those aerial motions which have rendered him so justly famous as a mariner of the air. As you lie amongst the tall brown heather, dreamily gazing upward into blue space, listening, it may be, to the humming of the passing insects, or the bleating of the lambs on the opposite hill-side, and the croak of the Ravens from the "Storr," your eye is riveted to a dark speck high in air, and looking no larger than a Crow. Nearer it comes; the shepherd who perchance is with you exclaims with almost bated breath "Iolair dhubh!" (the Black Eagle); and breathless you watch the king of birds explore the air. Nearer and nearer he comes until he is directly above you – now flapping his broad wings at irregular intervals, now with them fully expanded, gliding round and round, without giving them any perceptible motion, the tips of the primaries separated and

With a seven-foot span, the golden eagle is majestic.

turned upwards, and the tail ever and anon turned from side to side as a rudder. Although he seems so near, he is still well out of the range of the heaviest shot, and for some time he busies himself by surveying our reclining forms on the hillside below him. But, see! the pair of Ravens that are nesting in the "Storr" are uneasy at his presence, and sally out to mob, if they dare, their king. Although pirates the same as he, they evidently do not put much faith in the old proverb of "honour amongst thieves," and croaking fiercely forth their displeasure at his presence, one flies above him, the other beneath, and each tries to buffet him. But prudence forbids, and they content themselves with noisy clamour, which is increased, in seeming exultation and triumph, as the Eagle sweeps slowly onwards, rising higher as he goes to clear the neighbouring hills, and disappears over the summit to pursue his course over the adjoining valley. Follow him in imagination there; see him at last alight on yonder hoary crag, his favourite perch for a generation. Notice how gracefully he folds his long, broad wings, slightly drooping, his neck closely retracted, with its bright golden plumes glowing in the light. There he remains for hours basking in the

101

bright sunbeams, digesting his meal, and collecting his energies for a fresh foray upon the defenceless and the weak. That favourite perch has been used for years and years. In fine and storm the monarch of the mountain seeks that favoured rock-pinnacle, there to bask in summer, or cling, firm as the rock itself, whilst the storm and the sleet drive past in blinding fury.

William Macgillivray (*Rapacious Birds of Great Britain,* 1836) describes his own encounters with golden eagles, and how his attitude towards these regal birds radically altered over the years.

My first acquaintance with the Golden Eagle happened in the following manner. On the farm of Northtown, in Harris, at that time held by my uncle, great havock had been made among the lambs by the eagles, which resorted to that peninsula from all parts of the mainland, and from the neighbouring island of Shellay. Two pairs usually nestled on the high rocks at its western extremity, and several covered pits had been formed in their vicinity, in the manner described in the preceding pages. I had just commenced the use of the gun, under the guidance of my uncle, and had only as yet fired five shots; with the first of which I had riddled a table, with the second demolished a rock-pigeon, killed two with the third, and with the rest had done nothing to my credit as a marksman. The sixth was destined for a higher deed. Not finding any flesh or fish, recent or putrid, about the place, I laid hold of a white hen, to the legs of which I fastened a bit of twine and a wooden peg, filled one of my jacket-pockets with barleygrain, the other with old newspapers; and, taking the hen under my arm, and my gun on my shoulder, proceeded to the farther brow of the hill. There I fastened the bird to the turf by means of the peg, left her the barley, put a double charge of buck-shot into the gun, and shut myself up in the pit. Before I had been there an hour, the rain had made its way through the roof, the newspapers had ceased to amuse, and I had fallen into a sort of slumber, from which I was startled by a shrill scream. My first motion was to peep through the hole, when I beheld an eagle perched on the back of the hen, which crouched close to the ground in terror; my second was to raise to my shoulder the but of my gun, of which the muzzle lay in the aperture of the hut; and, at the moment when the eagle was in the act of raising his head, as if to inflict a blow upon his unresisting victim, I fired, and received a severe contusion on the cheek, the gun having been overcharged. Impatient to know the result, I raised the roof on my back, forced myself through it, and, running up to the place, found the eagle quite dead; the whole shot having entered its side. So, this is all, thought I; – an eagle is nothing wonderful after all.

Many years after, having ascended to the summit of one of the lofty mountains in the Forest of Harris, in search of plants (for I had by this time become a botanist), I stood to admire the glorious scene that presented itself, and enjoy the most intense of all delights – that of communion in the wilderness with the God of the Universe. I was on a narrow ridge of rock, covered with the Silene acaulis, whose lovely pink blossoms were strewn around; on one side was a rocky slope, the resort of the ptarmigan; on the other a rugged precipice, in the crevices of which had sprung up luxuriant tufts of Rhodiola rosea. Before me, in the west, was the craggy island of Scarp; toward the south stretched the rugged coast-line of Harris, margined on the headlands with a line of white foam; and, away to the dim horizon, spread out the vast expanse of the Atlantic Ocean, with the lonely isles of St Kilda on its extreme verge. The sun, descending in the clear sky, threw a glistening path of light over the waters, and tinged the ocean haze with purple. Suddenly there arose over the Atlantic a mass of light thin vapour, which approached with a gentle breeze, rolling and spreading around, and exhibiting the most beautiful changes of tint. When I had gazed until the fading light reminded me that my home for the night was four miles distant, I approached the edge of the precipice, and bent over it, when, from the distance of a few yards beneath, a Golden Eagle launched forth into the air. The scene, already sublime, was by the flight of the eagle rendered still more so, and, as I gazed upon the huge bird sailing steadily away beneath my feet, while the now dense masses of cloud rolled majestically over head, I exclaimed aloud "Beautiful!" The great God of heaven and earth, myself, his perverse but adoring subject, and the eagle, his beautiful but unenduring creature, were all in the universe of my imagination. Scenes like these might soften the obdurate, elevate the grovelling, convince the self-willed and unbelieving, and blend with universal nature the spirits that had breathed the chilling atmosphere of selfishness. Verily, it is good for one to ascend a lofty mountain; but he must go alone; and if he be there in the solemn stillness of midnight, as I have been, he will descend a better and a wiser man. Beautiful truly it is, to see the eagle sweeping aloft the hill side, sailing from one mountain to another, or soaring aloft in its circling flight until it seems to float in the regions of the thin white cirri, like the inhabitant of another world looking down upon our rebel

earth, as if desirous to visit it, but afraid to come within its con-
taminating influence.

Seebohm, in his lengthy essay about this great bird (in *A History
of British Birds*, 1885), includes a passionate plea for its
protection after finding a nest on the island of Skye.

The nest of the Eagle was in a little grass-covered cavity about midway
down the precipice, in a place where the rocks overhung, forming, as it
were, a natural roof to the nest. The only way of getting to the nest at all
practicable was from below; and after giving orders to the men, I and a
shepherd commenced climbing down the rocks to the grassy platform at
the base of the cliff. We were able to climb down some 400 feet without
the aid of ropes, a cool head being all that was required; and when about
some hundred feet or so from the eyrie, we awaited the arrival of the
rope from above which was to assist me to the nest. The nest was built
on a ledge of the cliffs, in a little grassy hollow, and was made externally
almost exclusively of heather and a few large sticks, the lining being
composed of dried fern-fronds, grass, and moss, in small quantities, and
large tufts of green herbage. The nest itself was not very large nor
deep; and the lining-materials were built quite close up to the wall of
rock behind. The materials of the nest were not much interwoven,
although they were very firm and solid. All round and about the place,
and in the nest itself, were quantities of animal remains, fur and
feathers, bones and decaying flesh of hares, grouse, and lambs; for the
two young eaglets were rapidly coming to maturity. They opened their
mouths, snapped their beaks, and retired to the further end of the nest;
yet otherwise seemed to bother themselves little at the intrusion. The
nest was a somewhat bulky structure too, perhaps some four or five feet
in diameter. And what a noble view there was to be had! surely the
Eagles were wise in choosing such a home. As I clung to the grassy face
of the cliff, stupendous and rugged, every object was taken in at a glance
– the sea beneath, the sky with its large masses of white clouds, the birds
and all, even the fleet of herring-boats fishing in the Minch, some
twenty miles away, and the bleak and rugged peaks of Rum and Canna,
whilst 'hull down' on the horizon the Long Island lay in gloomy
indistinctness, all serving to add a charm and a grandeur to the Eagle's
wild abode. What an impressive scene! how wild, and yet how
beautiful! Long may the Golden Eagle haunt the wild cliffs and
mountains of that rugged shore; for so long as he is there the crowning
object of its beauty is ensured! Surely it is worth an effort to preserve

this last remnant of a noble race – a bird which must be so closely connected with the Scotch, their traditions, and their literature for all time. Surely the few lambs or fawns the Eagle takes is but a cheap price for its preservation and maintenance in the land to which it is so noble an ornament. Before it be too late, Scotchmen, protect your national bird, the Eagle of your ancestors, and stay the cruel war waged by grouse-shooter, deer-stalker, sheep-farmer, and skin-collector – a war which will, ere long, play its part but too surely, and take the Eagle from your mountains for ever!

In *Days with the Golden Eagle* (1927), Seton Gordon wrote of an eyrie in a Scots pine.

The eagle as she broods on her eyrie in this country of wild primeval forest has an inspiring view. She looks across to the high tops and sees the early morning sun flood the snowy slopes with rosy light. She hears from the forest below her the soft bubbling notes of the amorous blackcock at their fighting-ground, and the wild clarion call of the missel-thrush as he greets the April dawn. Other sounds she hears: the hoarse bark of a hind, the curious sneezing cry of a capercaillie on some pine tree, the distant melody of curlew and golden plover on the brown moorland, the becking of a cock grouse as he shakes the frosty dew from his plumage. I remember once spending a night beside an eagle at the eyrie and seeing the first sun-flush burn upon her golden head, so that it was no longer golden but deep rose coloured; and so I like to picture that lonely eyrie on many calm, sunny dawns when spring is young and when all the life of the lonely upland places is commencing slowly to stir to the increasing power of the sun.

Then there are days when the noontide sun shines full into the eyrie; when, even in April, the forest seems to burn with a fierce, dry heat; when the red ants swarm up and down the eagle's tree, and each large, conical ant-hill is a mass of seething, feverish life. There are days, too, in April when the black wind from the north brings with it dry, powdery snow which drifts across the moorland at the fringe of the forest, and the pines commence to droop beneath their mantle of soft, clinging white. From time to time the eagle rises on her nest and shakes the snow from her dark plumage, then gazes fiercely over the dim world of white that might be some Polar waste from the bitter cold of the wind and the grey masses of fast-driven snow.

Leslie Brown held the view that the eagle's surroundings become as important as the bird in the observer's appreciation (*Eagles*, 1955), and this sentiment is echoed in Seton Gordon's work in *Days with the Golden Eagle* (1927).

How clear is the air above the forest between the April showers! How delightful is the perfume from the young birch leaves in the sun-gleams that follow the rain! In olden times the maidens of the Highlands used to distil a perfume from the leaves of the birch. But one fears that they would not now be content with so natural a scent.

In the spring sunshine the forest lochs sparkle. Here handsome goosander drakes swim with their mates or fly swiftly from one feeding-ground to another. In the reed-beds wigeon court, and from the heathery shores of the lochs the greenshank's wild, tuneful music drifts down upon the breeze.

Beside the clear, alder-fringed pools the willow hangs out golden catkins; on sunny slopes the broom has already clothed herself with orange-coloured blossoms.

From the eagle's home far up the hillside one looks through the dark clustered pines on to the loch below. At first there is brilliant sunshine, then a shower of drifting hail forms swiftly, and a rainbow of brilliant colours is thrown across the loch. Beneath the fir trees beside the eagle's eyrie innumerable blaeberry plants are unfolding their green leaves, and amongst the leaves one sees here and there the small, rosy flower which

The golden eagle has a more regal bearing than the white-tailed.

in time will become the succulent dark-blue berry so eagerly sought after by the birds – and by the human race also.

One April when the eagle had her eyrie in the forest I reached the nest at noon and, concealed behind a tree, looked down upon the small fir beside a hill stream where the eagle was brooding her two handsome eggs. Hour after hour she sat there, and except that once she preened the feathers of one great wing she never stirred. A heavy shower of hail and snow passed across the forest from the high hills to the west, and when the sun again appeared it shone upon a world of white. Upon the eagle's back drops of water sparkled in the sun as she breathed slowly and rhythmically. And then, sailing swiftly up the corrie came her mate. With a rush of wings he alighted upon the branch of a tree beside her and stood there in the sunshine, a very king amongst birds. For perhaps a couple of minutes he remained, then gave himself a great shake (just as a dog might have done), spread his broad wings and sailed away.

The flight of an eagle poses fascinating and controversial questions. Seton Gordon continues in the same book.

The soaring powers of the golden eagle are well known, but what I witnessed one April day will be believed with difficulty. I was standing on a hill slope just above a pine forest where a pair of golden eagles have their nest each year. The day was bitterly cold, and a strong breeze from the north was bringing heavy snow showers to the glen, while on the high tops the drifting snow was whirled high into the air. As I stood there the eagle's mate came over the ridge. He was flying low, but on seeing me commenced to mount. Leaning upon the wind he rose higher and higher. There was no perceptible movement of his dark wings, yet he mounted until he was invisible to the eye. The glass still revealed him – a dark speck against the blue vault of the sky – then some clouds crossed and hid him from my view, for he was far above them. What height must he have reached when he was invisible to my unaided eye? It is of course impossible to do more than surmise, but in the autumn of 1926 I was on Sgurr nan Gillean, one of the Black Cuillin of Skye, when an eagle rose from his perch on the topmost pinnacle and sailed above me. Knowing my own height and the height of the hill-top, I was able accurately to judge his distance above me, and at an elevation of 1500 feet he seemed quite a large bird. And so I would say that for the eagle to be invisible to the unaided eye he must be 8000 feet above the observer.

Although my own experience was an interesting one, a stalker friend of mine, John McIntosh, who was for some seasons watcher at the Corrour Bothy in the Forest of Mar, saw an eagle climb even higher than I did. The weather had been intensely hot on the Cairngorms, and then one day the north wind brought cool air to the hills. McIntosh happened to see a golden eagle soar out from its ledge of rock and "put the glass on to it," as they say in stalking language. This eagle, too, mounted serenely and without effort into the wind, and at last was so small that McIntosh could not see it with his unaided eye. But his glass for a time brought it nearer, and then even in the field of the telescope the bird was invisible. When it is remembered that a stalking-glass magnifies an object at least twenty-five times, it shows to what a great altitude that eagle had soared. It must have been at least ten thousand feet above the rock from which it took wing.

Part of the awe-inspiring quality of the eagle is the power it exhibits in attacking its prey. Colonel Meinertzhagen (*Pirates and Predators*, 1959) describes several eagle attacks.

In late September 1944 I was at Scourie in Sutherland. The cloud ceiling was low and rain was driving in from the south-west. Suddenly I heard the call of geese and looking up I saw a skein of seven grey-lag flying towards the sea and about 500 feet up. They were calling loud and often because one of their number had lagged behind and could be seen about fifty yards behind the main body. As I watched, and not over 200 yards from me, a golden eagle planed down through the clouds towards the laggard goose who was now honking blue murder and performing all sorts of zigzag evasive action in the hope of averting disaster. The eagle came up behind the goose and slightly below it, turned on his back and seized the bird from below with a smack which I clearly heard. The eagle must have got his talons well fixed in the goose for both fell in a tangled mass behind a rise and were lost to sight. I was too wet, tired and hungry to make any further investigation but have little doubt as to the end of that encounter. The main skein of geese, instead of bunching, as I had expected, scattered in every direction, registering their disapproval with loud honks. I was sorry for that lone goose.

Golden eagles are seldom successful after blue hares unless they come on them in soft snow or away from peat-hag country, the hare beating them by twists and turns in very broken country, where the eagle with his huge span and constant banking cannot flatten out low enough to seize his victim, his wing tips often scraping snow or peat, delaying speed and hindering quick turns. On one occasion I witnessed an eagle stoop at a hare on open snow over the flat of the bottom of a steep corrie. The hare made for broken ground but was brought up against a solid wall of snow and when the eagle was gaining fast and about to seize him under most favourable conditions, the hare suddenly turned just before the snow bank was reached and the eagle crash-dived into the snow, unable to check his speed and without room to turn. There was a small avalanche of powdered snow as the bewildered eagle extricated himself and sat for a moment dazed, abandoning hare-hunting for that afternoon. After shaking himself and sitting for a moment in uncertainty, he resumed his majestic pose and sailed down the corrie.

The question of damage done by eagles (and the consequent persecution of them) has already been touched upon. Seton Gordon's views in *Days with the Golden Eagle* (1927) are clear.

The amount of harm eagles do on a sheep-farm is very difficult to compute, and although some shepherds and sheep-farmers regard the eagle as the enemy of young lambs, I am convinced that it is only exceptionally that eagles take *living* lambs. The golden eagle is fond of carrion of all sorts, and a dead lamb on a dark hillside cannot fail to attract him. A certain number of lambs are born dead every spring, and when a snowstorm or much cold, wet weather is experienced during the lambing season the mortality is great. To see a lamb in an eagle's eyrie is sufficient proof to many shepherds that eagles are taking their living lambs. They do not stop to think whether the lamb was dead before it was carried to the eyrie. I shall always remember the fairness of one shepherd who showed me an eagle's eyrie in which no fewer than four lambs were lying. Far from showing signs of annoyance, the shepherd told me he was convinced that all these lambs had been dead when they had been taken by the eagle, for, he said, the mortality among lambs had been unusually great that spring. But would not the average shepherd, after seeing four lambs at an eyrie, have been the eagle's sworn enemy for life? On less evidence than this a friend of mine put a black mark against the pair of eagles that were nesting on his ground. A number of his lambs went amissing. A fox might have taken them, or they might have succumbed to any of the many dangers that beset the very young. My friend, however, was convinced that they had been killed by the eagles. Perhaps they had been so taken; more likely they had not. There was no proof either way.

Meinertzhagen was quite clear that honey buzzards primarily preyed upon wasps. He was also characteristically concerned about their protection (*Pirates and Predators*, 1959).

Does the honey buzzard get stung? The feathers on the face are stiff and coarse; it has been doubted whether they offer protection against the sting of a wasp. This sting when fully protruded does not exceed 2½ mm. and that of a hornet 3 mm. The weight of a wasp makes no impression on these short stiff feathers, and they are so arranged that no wasp sitting on them could possibly reach the skin.

It has been estimated that a single bird will kill 90,000 wasps in the season.

The honey buzzard bred in Britain in 1957. I knew the owner of the estate and the keeper; I was able to arrange complete protection from all kinds of disturbance. But both owner and keeper said "What about my pheasants?" To satisfy them I said honey buzzards did not molest pheasants, but if this pair did I would reward them 2s. 6d. a pheasant. The wretched birds took forty-seven pheasants. I also put up notices at the entrances to the wood "Unexploded bombs, keep out." It certainly kept people out but I got into trouble with the War Office for "alarming the public." This particular pair of honey buzzard reared three young who first took wing in late July. In addition to pheasants, the parents were seen on plough searching for insects and the remains of snails were found beneath the nest and in pellets.

When we come to the common buzzard, we lose most of the feeling of awe which so often accompanies stories of the golden eagle. William Macgillivray, however, in *Rapacious Birds of Great Britain* (1836), endeavoured to restore some of the balance.

The Buzzard seems somehow, no doubt quite unintentionally on his part, to have incurred the displeasure of ornithologists, few of whom have refrained from applying to him the most opprobrious epithets. Were we to credit all that has been said respecting him, we should take him to be a lazy, sleepy, cowardly fellow, who doses away half his time on some old rotten trunk, and who, even when hungry, cannot be persuaded to do more than look about him from his stand, and when some feeble or crippled object comes up, make an undecided plunge after it, or perhaps scramble by the side of a ditch to clutch a sprawling frog, or scratch among cow-dung for beetles and larvae. For my part, I cannot believe all that has been said to his disadvantage, and having a

Fortunately, in some areas the buzzard can still be counted as common.

kind of natural propensity to side with the weaker party, especially if it be the injured one, as it is almost always sure to be, I shall endeavour to reinstate the Buzzard in that respectability which Nature has accorded to him.

The red kite produces equally diverse responses – a coward, a scavenger, yet a master of the aerial environment. Macgillivray certainly appreciated it.

This beautiful and interesting bird is remarkable among our predatory species for its peculiar flight. The body being very light in proportion to the expanse of wings and tail, a buoyant, gliding, and rather unsteady flight is produced, which in some measure resembles that of the larger gulls, and especially the Lestris parasiticus. Birds of this character do not proceed by means of quick beatings of their wings, although their progress may occasionally be extremely rapid; and the kite, instead of flying like the peregrine or the wood pigeon, both heavy birds, but furnished with powerful wings and tail, moves along in beautiful curves and circlings, with scarcely perceptible motions of its wings, but balancing itself by means of its very long and expansile tail. It sometimes, like the Eagles and Buzzards, ascends to a vast height, and continues for a long time to sail in circles, apparently for the mere purpose of amusing itself, or of gently exercising its muscles, for the effort of ascending to his elevation cannot be in any degree comparable to that used even by a Highlander in ascending a hill, and the upper

111

fields of air once gained, the kite can float at ease and in security. But when searching for prey, it flies at the height of from thirty to a hundred feet, wending its curving way in gentle sweeps, constantly moving its partially expanded tail to either side, and slightly drawing in and extending its long wings. To quote the words of Buffon, who has well described the flight of the kite, "one cannot but admire the manner in which it is performed; his long and narrow wings seem immovable; it is his tail that seems to direct all his evolutions, and he moves it continually; he rises without effort, comes down as if he was sliding along an inclined plane; he seems rather to swim than to fly; he darts forwards, slackens his speed, stops, and remains suspended or fixed in the same place for whole hours, without exhibiting the smallest motion of his wings." There is a little exaggeration here, as is natural for a poet.

Poetical exaggeration is, happily, frequently applied to birds of prey! Guy Mountfort, writer of the famous *Portrait* series and the *Field Guide to Birds of Britain and Europe*, is not prone to exaggerate. His description of the red kite is all the more impressive for that (*Portrait of a Wilderness*, 1958).

The Kite is not only a complete master of the art of soaring and gliding, but is a most beautiful sight to watch in flight. To see one rise from the ground is to gain an impression of weak and laboured flight, but once it has climbed to a sufficient height, it spreads its "sails" and begins to soar in wide circles. The flexible primary wing-feathers open like sensitive fingers, seeking to gain maximum advantage from the eddying thermal currents. The graceful, deeply forked tail swings loosely from side to side, now closed, now open to its fullest extent, twisting at times unbelievably at right angles to the horizontal plane. Like the vultures, the Kite likes to sit on a favourite perch in the early mornings, waiting for the sun to heat the ground and bring forth the rising thermals. As its food is largely slow-moving prey and occasional carrion it has little need for speed in level flight. Nevertheless it succeeds in catching a variety of less agile mammals and birds, as well as snakes, lizards, fish, toads and frogs. Dragonflies are often caught in flight. Earth-worms are obviously considered a delicacy. With such large numbers of semi-wild cattle living on the Coto there is no shortage of carrion, though this is much less important to the Kite than to the Black Kite. Myxomatosis struck the region in 1955, but failed to wipe out the Rabbits, which evidently bred immunity to the disease and are today as numerous as ever, to the great benefit of Kites and other raptors.

For soaring and sailing flight, the red kite is unsurpassed.

Seen at close quarters, the Kite is a richly coloured bird of graceful proportions. Its pale head is strongly streaked with black, the eye being large, with an amber iris, and the hooked bill is delicately shaped by comparison with an eagle's. The body is a rich reddish brown, the feathers of the upper parts being boldly edged with buff. The long, angular wings have black primaries, with large and conspicuous whitish patches beneath. The very long swallow-tail is a rich, pale chestnut.

David Bannerman was equally eloquent in his description of red kites in the Canary Islands (*The Birds of the British Isles,* 1956).

I well remember one glorious day at Maspalomas in the south of Grand Canary watching a fleet of native fishing boats heading for the shore. The sky was cloudless and brilliantly blue and not a bird was in sight save a solitary raven flying along the coast-line while uttering its deep throaty croak. As the leading boat ran aground there appeared, literally out of the blue, a dozen or more red kites which, perhaps beyond

113

human sight, had been watching the fleet heading for land, knowing what was in store. The great birds just dropped from the heavens and within a few minutes were flying screaming round the boats as the fish were gutted. They reminded me of gulls crowding round the stern of a liner, jostling and fighting amongst themselves for every morsel thrown into the sea. It was a remarkable sight to anyone familiar with the kite's usual wariness, even when feeding on carrion washed up on the shore.

The powers of flight of the kite are difficult to beat even by the vulture, and in the clear atmosphere of the Canary Islands can be seen to perfection; in the Cumbres of Grand Canary, where extensive views are obtained, one or more kites is seldom out of sight. I have watched individual birds soaring upwards in great spiral curves until they appear but specks in the sky and during these manoeuvres the tail is clearly used as a rudder. Each pair of kites was observed to have their own territory, over which they would beat backwards and forwards, but that is probably only in the breeding season, for one cannot imagine a bird of its wing-power allowing itself to be unduly confined. More often in the winter time they are encountered sailing along the barren hillsides in huge curves, covering a great area with very little effort. When the wings are used they move with a slow beat.

The kites in the Canaries are used to good weather, and rain and mist have a depressing effect on them. At such times the birds will seek out some old dead tree and sit for hours on end in thoroughly dejected mood, feathers ruffled and head sunk low between the shoulders. I found that they continually returned to the same roosting places, choosing habitually very high pines. At such times they are difficult to approach and, being gifted with astonishing eyesight, are not easily taken by surprise.

Red kites soar and glide; peregrines fly in an altogether different way. To many eyes, however, they are as impressive as any bird of prey. T. A. Coward (*The Birds of the British Isles and their Eggs*, 1969) described them very well.

There is a dash, neatness and finish in the flight of the Peregrine which is purely its own. The wings move rapidly, beating the air for a few moments, and are then held steady in a bow whilst the bird glides forward, sometimes rolling slightly from side to side. The legs, as in other raptorial birds, lie under the tail and are not held forward except when striking; at times one leg will be dropped and shaken during flight. When seen from above the bird looks blue, from below, red or rufous, but if at a distance or high in the air it looks a black arc or swiftly moving crescent. The bend of the bow varies with the speed and inclination of flight; during descent, when the wing tips point backward, it is a sharp curve. Near a coastwise eyrie the bird will sail out over the water, easily and gracefully, rising to a great height, then with wings almost closed shoot seaward, recovering itself near the water and after a low flight above the waves mount once more. Tiercel and falcon, as the male and female are called, join in aerial gambols, sporting together as one or the other playfully mounts and stoops at its consort. The "stoop" of the Peregrine is its swoop or downward rush with almost closed wings, seen to best advantage when hunting. An aerial fight between two tiercels is a sight to be remembered; the stoops and dodges are no play then; the birds rise to a great height, each striving to get above the other to gain advantage for the stoop, which is avoided often by a sudden upward rush of the lower bird, accompanied by a scream of rage or fear. In one such fight neither bird succeeded in striking, but the turns, twists and ruses to avoid impact by the one which happened to be below were wonderful to watch.

The methods of hunting and killing used by peregrines have always caused much speculation and comment. Meinertzhagen (*Pirates and Predators*, 1959) saw many interesting episodes, including the following.

In level flight a peregrine will bind to the victim, seizing neck or body and carrying; or it will sometimes turn underneath its prey and seize the stomach; but these techniques are only used with birds considerably less than its own weight. The normal method is a stoop at terrific speed, when the victim is hit with either one or both hind claws; the probable aim is the head or neck, in which case the head of the victim has been known to fall a hundred yards from the body; but more often the victim is disabled by a deep gash on the back or by a broken wing.

A peregrine's technique is so varied that I give some cases I have witnessed.

In Arabia in 1948 I came across eight of the large chukar (*Alectoris melanocephala*) watering in a close bunch in the open. A peregrine came up the wadi, catching them in the open; the chukar crouched; the hawk made shallow stoops at them on the ground; these proving ineffectual, he settled about twenty yards from them; but some inquisitive baboon aproached, jabbering and fussing to such an extent that the falcon flew off; how that attack might have ended is uncertain.

Many people rate the peregrine as the most exciting of all birds.

In Hampshire I have seen a peregrine stoop at a covey of partridges to try and make them rise, but after each stoop, and during the time the hawk was preparing for his next stoop, the partridges would move slightly nearer some dense bushes until they were so close as to run off into them before the hawk could turn. I have also seen a peregrine alight in heather and deliberately hunt for grouse which refused to fly, and eventually catch one on the ground.

As a boy I lived in the Test Valley. In hard weather duck of all sorts would congregate on flooded land and ponds and these duck were always accompanied by a pair of peregrine; every evening they harried the duck, preferring wigeon to mallard or teal. Killing was carried out by stoop, always over dry land, and the pair of hawks were amazingly successful, rarely failing at their first attempt. In the still frosty air we always heard a resounding smack as the hawk struck and then watched the spiral dive to the dead victim lying in the water meadow.

I have on several occasions seen peregrine after teal but never with complete success. On the first occasion, in Kenya, the teal just managed to dive into reeds at such speed that he was temporarily stunned and was caught. On the second occasion, in Baluchistan, a teal, closely followed by a peregrine, dived at full speed into deep water; the hawk banked, hovered over the spot and picked up the teal from the surface when he showed and flew off with it. The third occasion was in Caithness, when a peregrine stooped at a small party of teal in a peat pond surrounded by buck-bean and reeds. The hawk continued to hover over the teal who were more terrified of the peregrine than they were of us, for nothing would induce them to rise even when a dog was put in after them. They were quacking their poor souls out. On the following day we saw a peregrine stoop at and bind to a grouse. One of the covey lost its head and dived headlong into thick heather whence he was picked up half-stunned.

On a cold clear November day I was on the summit of Mount Hekla in South Uist; much cackling announced the autumn arrival of hundreds of barnacle geese flying high overhead at about 5000 feet, and a pair of peregrine seemed to be amusing themselves by stooping at them, whether in earnest or play we shall never know, but the geese considered it serious, and many side-slipping or with almost vertical dive descended to Loch Bee, the two hawks continually harassing them right down to the water level.

Dixon, quoted by Henry Seebohm in *A History of British Birds* (1885), narrates the effects of Peregrines upon puffins:

Dixon, writing of the Peregrine on Skye, says: – "A favourite morsel with the Peregrine is the comical little Puffin, or 'Sea-Parrot,' as the fishermen call him; in fact in some localities this bird almost forms his only food. Here, for instance, on this steep ocean-cliff a colony of Puffins have established themselves. The time is early morning; and the Puffins are coming to and quitting their holes, from and to the sea below, where quite a large company are fishing and disporting themselves. Several of the curious little birds leave the cliff together, and with rapid beats of their short wings pass to the water below. Suddenly a loud flapping of wings is heard, *something* flits like a meteor from the air above, and follows the Puffins in their downward course. Perceiving their danger they scatter; but too late; already one of their number is struck and quivering in the sharp talons of their common enemy. All for the moment is commotion: the birds on the sea beneath dive out of danger; and those on the cliffs are in uproar at the suddenness of the onslaught. But the alarm soon subsides, and the birds are pursuing their usual avocations again. Indeed it is a noteworthy fact that the birds display very little alarm whilst the Falcon sails high in air above them; and it is no uncommon thing to see the bird, evidently when its appetite is satisfied, surrounded by Terns and Gulls, and see the Puffins sitting quite unconcerned a stone's throw from their enemy."

117

In some ways, merlins have been likened to miniature peregrines. Meinertzhagen (*Pirates and Predators*, 1959) tells of the antics of merlins.

They are lively, audacious, marvellously active and usually fly close to the ground. They also have an impertinent side to their character. I witnessed a cock merlin in Mull chasing a meadow pipit which took refuge between the legs of a grazing cart-horse. There was a scurry and chase between the legs of the horse who strongly resented the scrimmage about its person; but the pipit escaped; the merlin flew away disgusted, but after going about twenty yards suddenly turned and deliberately struck the poll of the horse, causing it to throw up its head in alarm; having accomplished this act of spiteful bad manners the merlin flew off. This act reminds me of a story related by an eccentric gentleman I met at lunch with Lord Allenby in Sinai during the First World War. He said with great seriousness that he had seen a merlin strike a cart-horse senseless to the ground. Allenby, with a twinkle in his eye but with great seriousness, said that his experience had been that when anger entered into the soul of a wild animal, it became irresponsible, for in South Africa he had seen a wild cat, disturbed in its siesta by a large bull giraffe, pounce on the enormous beast, climb rapidly up its neck and tear its throat out.

The kestrel is less dashing as a rule, but it does have the considerable benefit of at least being common in areas where other birds of prey, for one reason or another, are virtually absent. Its behaviour attracted the attention and admiration of Henry Seebohm (*A History of British Birds*, 1885).

From its habit of hovering in the air, the Kestrel is probably the best-known and most easily recognized of all British raptorial birds. This peculiarity has gained for it the colloquial name of windhover. It hangs in the air, poised over one spot, with outspread wings and tail, as if suspended by a thread. Seldom, indeed, can one take a walk in the country without making a passing acquaintance with this graceful little Falcon. A favourite locality for the Windhover is in rocky valleys: the dales of the Peak of Derbyshire are one of its favourite haunts, where it nestles in the lofty limestone cliffs. Amongst all the dales and moors and rocks of Yorkshire its pretty gambols in the air, its wonderful evolutions and graceful movements, form one of the most charming accessories of the wild impressive scenery of many parts of this county.

In most of England, the kestrel is the only regularly-seen bird of prey.

Easily distinguished, indeed, it is from all others of its order; and its presence is readily detected as it hovers in the air

> "As if let down from the heaven there
> By a viewless silken thread,"

now advancing towards you, flying up wind, some thirty feet above the earth, its wings flapping hurriedly or held perfectly motionless. Now it is directly above you; you see its broad head turning restlessly from side to side; the wings seem in a perpetual quiver, and the broad tail is expanded to its fullest extent. Now it glides slowly forward for a few yards, pauses for a moment intently surveying the ground beneath, then once more, with a few vigorous flaps of its wings, darts off in a sidelong direction, and poises itself in the air as before. Again it proceeds a little distance, hovers, and bounds forward. Then, by describing a broad circle, it turns completely round, and flies rapidly down wind, but soon suddenly stops and hovers again. Something has arrested its attention; a mouse is below it in the meadow-grass; and, closing its wings, it drops like a stone, throwing out its wings again just before it reaches the earth, hovers a moment, clutches its prey, and as rapidly mounts the air, and bears off in direct and rapid flight to some quiet haunt, where it can devour its prey in peace. Sometimes you may see it at a stupendous height, wheeling round and round in circles; and when passing from one place to another it usually does so at a considerable height.

David Bannerman (*The Birds of the British Isles*, 1956) perhaps preferred lesser kestrels.

The 18th of February 1951 will remain in my memory as a red-letter day for lesser kestrels. We were then exploring the Forêt de la Marmora in western Morocco and on entering a glade of the forest we saw no less than ten lesser kestrels in a single tree and others close at hand which had obviously just arrived, as we had been walking in that forest for a week without sign of a bird. Then, all of a sudden, the glades were alive with them, gliding in turn from the branches to the ground, where they were feverishly engaged in devouring grasshoppers. In the bright sunlight the heads of the males looked wonderfully blue, and as they descended to the ground they spread their blue-grey tails and exhibited the broad white tips to all the rectrices. A few hours later our way took us to the mouth of the Mehdia River and there we had the delight of finding the lesser kestrels in solitary possession of an old ruined castle which overlooks the estuary. Many of the birds were sitting quietly on the ancient battlements, making occasional flights over the water, while others soared above the ruin. Against the clear blue sky these birds looked very lovely, so gracefully did they fly and so clean and fresh was their plumage. We were soon to find them preparing to nest in a high wall overlooking the shore, flanking a single-track railway. This wall was honeycombed with holes, while circling in the air above, or flying out over the estuary, were literally dozens of lesser kestrels, all obviously watching for our departure, as we were the only disturbing feature in an otherwise deserted landscape. We made as if to depart then sat down to watch, and all at once the birds came pouring in. Each swooped into its hole; sometimes several entered the same aperture but within two minutes the air was empty of birds and from every hole protruded a lesser kestrel's tail. A little owl, perched on a wall close to where we were sitting, seemed as interested a spectator as we were ourselves of this truly astonishing sight. The kestrels shot into the holes as quickly and as adroitly as the white-bellied swifts we were to see doing the same thing in the walls of Fez. Only now and again would a bird cling for a moment to the entrance with outspread tail and half-folded wing, occasionally to take another flight over the sea before finally entering its resting place. At such moments a glimpse of the white claws might be obtained as a bird fluttered against the wall. There must have been quite a hundred birds in the vicinity.

Bannerman was not nearly so enamoured of marsh harriers, but his observations on these birds in the same book nevertheless make interesting reading.

The marsh harriers beat steadily to and fro, with strong purposeful flight, their bright eyes ever searching the ground beneath for any suspicious movement in the swamp. The month was August and the young harriers must already have been abroad, but those which we saw so meticulously quartering the marsh were all old birds and, if I recollect rightly, mostly males. Every now and again a bird would arrest its flight and drop out of sight in the swamp with a corkscrew turn of the wings as if struck by a charge of shot. A frog may have been the cause of the sudden plunge or perhaps an immature coot. These harriers must be the terror of every marsh bird for miles around and in the nesting season they are constantly mobbed by redshanks and lapwings whose young, together with those of coots, moorhens and ducks, they so often destroy.

Hen Harriers occupy different ground, at least in summer. Kenneth Richmond in *Wild Venture* (1958) understandably finds them irresistible.

For the moment I took it for the sub-song of a Redwing. The soft, chortling notes were somehow familiar – vaguely thrush-like – and yet for the life of me I could not place them. It was a raw, cheerless day, as grey as they come in November, past four in the afternoon and the light failing. Still the notes continued, quietly reflective rather than subdued, a lively ditty full of starts and stops. The only birds in sight were some Redwings and Fieldfares which had crowded into the top of a rowan bush beside the burn; and they, so far as I could see, were all busy, snatching and gulping the berries as if their lives depended upon it. Not a songster among them.

How easily the ear is deceived! The ventriloquist turned out to be a Dipper which had ensconced itself in the bankside and which flew out, almost under my feet, zit-zitting to itself as it shot off upstream. At this the Fieldfares chattered a warning and took off in a body, only to settle again in the field a furlong or so away. The last of them was hardly down when a dove-grey hawk came breasting low over the rise, light as a puff of air. A cock Hen Harrier, indolent-looking as ever. It was over and on them before they could move. In a trice it sideslipped and pinned the nearest Fieldfare to the ground.

The incident was over in a twinkling, as neat as a slip catch taken on the half turn. There was no chance, no twisting and turning of pursuer and pursued, hardly a pounce even. The trick was done at the drop of a hat, with the consummate ease of a master of legerdemain; and though, for once in a lifetime, I was lucky enough to be the right spot at the right time it was hard to say just what happened. How easily the eye is taken unawares! The thrust was quicker than thought.

With its wing held loose and its tail spread, the Harrier shrouded its victim and was about to pluck it when the cry of a passing Crow caused it to look up.

Kra-ark! shouted the Crow accusingly, circling overhead.

No peace for the wicked! Rather than have its meal disturbed the Harrier rose at once, yikkering in annoyance, and continued on its line of flight as if nothing had happened. Like all hawks, it carried its prey slung beneath its tail. But for some reason (either because it was not hungry or because the kill was too heavy, or maybe because in its nervous haste it had failed to clutch it securely), the Harrier had not flown twenty yards before it let the bundle fall. I saw where it pitched in the grass, rolling over, its wings still flapping. Graceful and buoyant now, alternately flapping and sailing as if it had all the time in the world, the Harrier made off across the heather and was soon lost in the haze.

To cross the burn and run to the stricken Fieldfare was the work of a moment, but the bird was already dead by the time I reached it. All but one of its tail feathers had been torn off and blood was oozing from its bill. There were claw marks on the head, and the lower half of the body had been well and truly transfixed. Warm and limp, the little corpse lay in my hand, its eyes still bright, its richly coloured breast feathers unruffled. Its crop was as firm as a well-fed pigeon's, stuffed full, no doubt, of rowan berries.

What is the appropriate emotion for such occasions, I wonder? Pity for a wasted life? Hardly that, seeing that it made so clean an ending. Anger at a cold-blooded killing? Not that, either, seeing that the execution was so swift and carried out with such adroitness. Standing there in the gloom I was filled with admiration and, yes, with a fierce joy: for this was no ordinary act of violence that I had been privileged to witness but a feat of incomparable skill performed by an aristocrat. For a bird-watcher it was, you might say, the moment of truth.

As David Bannerman describes in *The Birds of the British Isles* (1956), hen harriers are often the focus of angry avian activity – and also have spectacular displays.

Hen-harriers when hunting are frequently mobbed by other birds. Nethersole-Thompson recalls one male harrier which used to work a hillside on which was a nesting colony of lesser black-backed gulls and while it was quartering the ground the gulls deafened the ear with their hoarse cries and fell like snowflakes upon the big blue hawk, which neither called nor retaliated but pursued the even tenor of its way. Curlews also harass the hen-harrier, while a merlin rarely misses an opportunity of dashing at the larger bird. A cock merlin is particularly aggressive when harrier and merlin are both nesting in the same valley. Then, the cock merlin throws himself with eager dashing flight at the harrier. One moment he is high in the air, and the next swooping straight and true at the gliding form beneath him. The merlin's excited screams sometimes draw his mate from her eggs. Then the two little falcons will stoop, check and throw up, as they buzz round the harrier like a pair of angry hornets. When merlins, short-eared owls and hen-harriers are neighbours many a great battle takes place.

Of the beautiful spring flight of the hen-harrier – the "dance", as one writer calls it – much has been written, and it is certainly one of the most remarkable spectacles of the bird world. On a sunny morning in May the gull-blue male leaves the scrub with an odd flight which recalls that of a tern, his wings at times almost touching each other beneath his breast. Then, having gained height, he will soar over the marsh for a while. Suddenly he mounts almost vertically with strong, swift wing-beats, to as suddenly drop headlong, with wings pressed to his body, towards the scrub below. Recovering, the ecstatic bird rises steeply again, and once more plunges down in a breath-taking dive. Before closing his handsome, black-tipped wings, he may turn onto one side, or even somersault, and all the time he calls to his mate circling beneath him. And so the dance continues over the marsh. Sometimes the ringtail herself "dances". The sky may be overcast, and a cutting wind searching the marsh, but still the brown hawk circles above the willow brake that will later hold her nest. There she tumbles in the air, falling like a plummet, swinging up, somersaulting, and falling again.

Like so many other species, hen harriers take on an extra degree of attraction because of the places they inhabit. William Macgillivray knew this well (*Rapacious Birds of Great Britain*, 1836).

Should we, on a fine summer day, betake us to the outfields bordering an extensive moor, on the sides of the Pentland, the Ochill, or the Peebles Hills, we might chance to see the harrier, although hawks have been so much persecuted that one may sometimes travel a whole day without meeting so much as a kestrel. But we are now wandering amid thickets of furze and broom, where the blue milkwort, the purple pinguicula, the yellow violet, the spotted orchis, and all the other plants that render the desert so delightful to the strolling botanist, peep forth in modest beauty from their beds of green moss. The golden plover, stationed on the little knoll, on which he has just alighted, gives out his

Hen harriers capture the spirit of the moorlands they inhabit.

shrill note of anxiety, for he has come, not to welcome us to his retreats, but if possible to prevent us from approaching them, or at least to decoy us from his brood; the lapwing, on broad and dusky wing, hovers and plunges over head, chiding us with its querulous cry; the whinchat flits from bush to bush, warbles its little song from the top-spray, or sallies forth to seize a heedless fly whizzing joyously along in the bright sunshine. As we cross the sedgy bog, the snipe starts with loud scream from among our feet, while on the opposite bank the gor cock raises his scarlet-fringed head above the heath, and cackles his loud notes of anger or alarm, as his mate crouches amid the brown herbage.

But see, a pair of searchers not less observant than ourselves have appeared over the slope of the bare hill. They wheel in narrow curves at the height of a few yards; round and round they fly, their eyes no doubt keenly bent on the ground beneath. One of them, the pale blue bird, is now stationary, hovering on almost motionless wing; down he shoots like a stone; he has clutched his prey, a young lapwing perhaps, and off he flies with it to a bit of smooth ground, where he will devour it in haste. Meanwhile his companion, who is larger, and of a brown colour, continues her search; she moves along with gentle flappings, sails for a short space, and judging the place over which she has arrived not unlikely to yield something that may satisfy her craving appetite, she flies slowly over it, now contracting her circles, now extending them, and now for a few moments hovering as if fixed in the air. At length, finding nothing, she shoots away, and hies to another field; but she has not proceeded far when she spies a frog by the edge of a small pool, and, instantly descending, thrusts her sharp talons through its sides. It is soon devoured, and in the mean time the male comes up. Again they fly off together; and were you to watch their progress, you would see them traverse a large space of ground, wheeling, gliding, and flapping, in the same manner, until at length, having obtained a supply of savoury food for their young, they would fly off with it.

The sparrowhawk is of a different design and quite unlike any of the other raptors so far considered in its habits and habitat. Henry Seebohm's essay in *A History of British Birds* (1885) remains useful and instructive.

From the nature of his food, the Sparrow-Hawk is seldom found in the wildest districts; there his place is taken by the Merlin. His haunt is the lowland woods and coppices or the fir-clumps on the borders of the moorlands – the rich well-cultivated lands on which game abounds, interspersed with woods and plantations: this is the Sparrow-Hawk's favourite home, where the food of his choice is found in great abundance. Although he frequently takes his station on the ground, or more often on a tree or fence, or on a stone wall or rock-ledge, using these situations as points of observation, the air is his province, and his flight in some respects stands almost unrivalled amongst birds. When seeking his food he flies down the wood-side, silently and swiftly gliding along just above the ground. If he sees you as he passes, with incredible speed he swerves into the cover, threading his way amongst the tangled network of branches gracefully and unharmed, to emerge a little distance further down and pursue his search as before. Often he will tarry for a moment above a clump of wild roses or brambles: mayhap a Robin is there; but he hops into cover in time to cheat his enemy. Onwards again flies the Sparrow-Hawk, now bounding over a fence, now gliding rapidly down the side of the cover, shooting and turning from side to side, or ever and anon rising in a beautiful curve over a hedge, scanning its further side, then back again. Perhaps a Thrush is started, and the relentless Hawk pursues it; but the Thrush is often too quick, or the Hawk mayhap is not hungry; for it gains a thick bush and its pursuer passes on, to sweep lightly upwards and perch on some decaying ivy-grown stump, standing erect and motionless, surveying the ground around him. Again he takes the air, leisurely at first, but with a quick swerve to the left, descending as he goes, he strikes a small bird, sitting quite unconscious of danger on a topmost twig, and bears it off in an instant into the wood from which he emerged but a short half-hour before. The amazing swiftness with which the Sparrow-Hawk takes its prey, and the dexterity with which it threads its way through the branches at its fullest speed, are quite beyond the powers of written description; they must be witnessed to be fully appreciated. How often does the rush of its wings disturb your reverie, as you are, mayhap, watching some little chorister a few yards away! and before you have time for thought, the little creature in whom you were so interested is quivering in death-agony in the talons of this warrior bird. Your presence seems totally disregarded, and the Hawk appears only to see its intended victim. But its swoop is not always attended with success; and probably far more birds escape than are taken when the chase is a prolonged one. Dixon has, amongst many other notes, one to the effect that he was on one occasion observing a Robin engaged in song, when a Sparrow-Hawk struck at it, but missed its intended victim, which at once took refuge with loud cries of alarm in the densest part of the thicket. It may be that the sudden sight of

With reduced use of certain pesticides, the sparrowhawk is making a comeback.

man disconcerted the Hawk, and caused it to miss its prey. On another occasion he witnessed one of these hawks pursue a Blue Titmouse for fully fifty yards up a fence; when the little creature, calling loudly all the time, at last managed to gain the shelter of a thick bush. In this instance, however, the Hawk perched near at hand, and appeared to be waiting for its quarry to again come forth into the open, until it was driven reluctantly away by an incautious movement on the part of its observers. The moment a bird is pursued it endeavours to seek safety in some dense cover which the Hawk cannot penetrate, and which no amount of fluttering on the part of the Hawk will cause it to quit when once safely reached. Numerous, indeed, are the instances on record of this bird's boldness and rapacity, it being almost impossible to read any account of this species without coming across some fresh instance of its daring.

Seebohm specifically mentions robin, treecreeper and wren amongst the sparrowhawk's victims – but Meinertzhagen muses on their relative immunity (*Pirates and Predators*, 1959).

The immunity of tits, tree-creepers, nuthatches, robins and wrens is remarkable; nor do these victims appear much in literature. Robins have only been recorded as victims when on migration and away from their usual habitat, and I have no record of a wren being taken, though I once saw in Cornwall an unsuccessful hunt in stone-wall country. A wren suddenly bobbed up with his challenging paean of self-satisfaction which soon altered to the *tic-tic* of alarm as he saw a sparrowhawk flying low in his direction. Down popped the wren into the loose stones and the hawk settled on the wall exactly where the wren had vanished. Up popped the wren not ten feet from the hawk, another *tic-tic*, and he was gone again before the hawk moved. Another pop-up, this time about ten yards from the hawk, another *tic-tic* and back into the wall. The hawk realised the game and made off. But the troglodyte was not satisfied with such an ending. He popped up for the last time to celebrate the victory, pouring out his soul in a paean of superiority and contempt for all predators.

Before leaving birds of prey, we should return to the warm Mediterranean lands where the numbers and diversity of species so much impress observers used to the limited fare available in Britain. It is difficult to resist Guy Mountfort's excitement at seeing short-toed eagles – surely one of the best of the eagles with its glorious expression, gleaming white underparts and impressive flight – especially at close range from a hide in Andalusia (*Portrait of a Wilderness*, 1958).

Seen at close quarters from the hide the large eyes of the adult eagles were startling in their extraordinary brilliance. They are a vivid, luminescent orange-yellow and quite unlike those of any other eagle. The plumage of both birds was unusually handsome, the bold horizontal markings on the flanks being particularly striking and darker than normal.

On the second visit of the male the nestling immediately seized the dangling tail of the snake which protruded from its bill and began pulling. The parent assisted the process of disgorgement with its foot, but the nestling did not release its hold during the tug-of-war which resulted. With quick backward motions of its head it began swallowing the 2-ft. snake, tail first. It was, however, soon obliged to regurgitate and to begin again, head first. In an astonishingly short space of time it engulfed the whole snake, although its own total length at that age was scarcely 10 in. But an even more amazing performance was filmed on another occasion. The male carried to the nest a snake nearly 3 ft. in length and 1½in. thick at its widest part. This was received by the female, who began tearing off tiny pieces for the nestling; but the latter

The short-toed eagle combines power and bold pattern with great grace.

soon got hold of the snake and began swallowing it. After gobbling the first 8 in. at a tremendous rate, it began choking and had to disgorge. It quickly began again, gulping at a steady rate of once every three to four seconds. By the time it reached the thickest part of the snake its tiny bill was stretched open to its fullest extent and the weight of the carcase made it fall over on its side. Hanging on grimly, it righted itself and continued its gargantuan meal, but pausing now from time to time in complete exhaustion. At the end of thirty-seven minutes the tip of the snake's tail finally disappeared and the nestling collapsed, its downy crop distended to half the size of its tiny body. Three and a half hours later it cheerfully ate another snake! The rapidity of the digestive processes of the young eagle was obviously phenomenal.

Imperial eagles look much like golden eagles in a field guide illustration (less so in real life), but their habits and behaviour are quite different. Andalusia provided Mountfort with many opportunities to watch them.

There was scarcely a day when we did not observe the Spanish Imperials either quartering the skies on the watch for prey, or indulging in magnificent aerobatics. Play is an essential function to most birds of prey and is part of the training of the young. During all three expeditions we saw adults obviously enjoying games. On one occasion a pair had been circling each other slowly at a great height, as though sparring for an opening; one then succeeded in getting behind the other and immediately a game of tag developed. First one and then the other

129

gained a position from which it could dive on its partner. At the conclusion of the final attack the lower bird rolled over on its back and seized the outstretched talons of the other. Thus interlocked and crying loudly they fell several hundred feet. They then separated, zoomed upwards again and repeated the process with every indication of enjoyment. Such play is, of course, often a "displacement activity" resulting from human trespass, as James Ferguson-Lees has proved with Peregrines. But some of our observations were made when the eagles were probably unaware of our presence. Other spectacular aerobatics which we saw were the result of territorial conflicts between neighbouring pairs.

One group, above all, of the raptors produces feelings complicated by contradictory emotional responses – the vultures. Vultures are both magnificent (none more so than griffons) and repulsive; both awe-inspiring and 'disgusting'. Fittingly, the literature on birds has plenty of glorious descriptions of both aspects. The bearded vulture, or lammergeier, is a rare and romantic bird. Meinertzhagen describes it in *Pirates and Predators* (1959).

Let me quote from my diary of 26 July 1914, on the eve of the First World War, when I found myself in the mountains of Baluchistan:

The finest view I ever had of a lammergeier occurred today. I came on him but a few feet away silhouetted against a gold-red sunset, magnificent against a horizon stretching for miles amd miles into golden infinity. He was quite unconscious of my presence. He sat on a rocky pinnacle facing the setting sun, wings slightly drooping and half-stretched head turned up towards heaven. Was this the phoenix of the ancients, Pliny's bird of brilliant golden plumage around the neck, the throat adorned with a crest and the head with a tuft of feathers? Was this lammergeier conscious of his sacred relationship with the sun? The phoenix of the ancients presaged peace everywhere in the land. What I saw this evening semed to foretell war, a long, bloody war. It was the finest, most beautiful and yet most terrible, the most romantic, view of any bird I have seen at any time anywhere.

Mountfort is undeniably a fan of vultures. He airs his opinions in *Portrait of a Wilderness* (1958).

I am not one who subscribes to the popular judgment that vultures are horrible creatures. There is a fascination in watching these great birds at close quarters and their mastery of soaring flight is always a source of wonderment. Their service to mankind throughout those parts of the world which they occupy is of inestimable value. Indeed without these greedy scavengers, to which nothing comes amiss, a great part of the over-populated tropics and semi-tropics might well be almost uninhabitable. They provide the only *corps sanitaire* in many regions where human survival is precariously balanced against disease and pestilence.

Bannerman found griffon vultures, in particular, very impressive (*The Birds of the British Isles*, 1956).

A first encounter with this bird outside a zoo is sure to remain fixed in one's memory. The experience fell to me in the Tell Atlas of Algeria when wandering up a narrow glen leading from the great Gorge du Chiffa, famed for its semi-tame Barbary apes. A passing shadow directed my gaze upwards and there, floating majestically above the high walls of the defile, were five griffons which I had inadvertently disturbed from their ledge. The breadth of their wings with pinions upturned and the short widespread tails at once proclaimed their identity, though I had never seen one before under such circumstances. As they peered down their light-coloured ruffs were clearly visible to the naked eye but soon they were mounting higher and higher, with barely a tilting of the great wings, until they had reached such a height that I could barely follow them with binoculars. I have seen griffons in many lands since that day and under many different circumstances but that first view of these huge birds at comparatively close quarters has never faded from my mind.

Griffons love the sun and hate the rain, and when caught in a downpour present rather a miserable appearance as they crouch on boulders with draggled wings and feathers. I well remember one February morning coming upon a party of thirty-five in the hills of Andalusia when on the road to Tarifa. The sun had come out after a heavy shower and the huge birds were sitting about the rock-strewn hillside drying their feathers in the sun. Some had their wings outspread in the manner of a cormorant which has emerged from the sea to dry its wings on a fish-trap. Under such circumstances griffons on the ground make an attractive picture but equally they can be repulsive when engaged in feeding, and a too close scrutiny of their behaviour at such times can make an observer feel quite sick.

Robert Atkinson, on an undergraduate expedition to south-west Spain with the object of photographing griffons at the nest, also found them awesome creatures. His account (in *Quest for the Griffon*, 1938) shows that the sudden arrival of a bird at the nest, a few feet from the hide, was a memorable moment.

No sign of any vultures. Can just see Mediterranean round on left.... My God, bird behind (No. 1.) just arrived. What a size! Heard a scratching noise – talons on rock – screwed round and saw her head only. Then she lowered her head between her shoulders and waddled on to the nest. Shuffled over egg like an enormous broody hen. She isn't four feet behind me and her eye seems to pierce straight through the hide, and me. Can't see her very distinctly except for fluffy white neck ruff and close down on head – looks quite clean. Huge hooked grey bill and yellow and black eye. Wind is blowing her tail up. She must see me. There're only a few straggling bits of broom across the peephole between her and me. She keeps turning her head from side to side but doesn't seem nervous; though I do. She blinks often and incredibly rapidly – eye just goes opaque for a fraction of a second. Her head seems nearly all bill, and upper mandible at that. She is most intrigued by hide and examines every inch of it. Wind seems nearly to lift her off the egg. She looks clean and well groomed, not at all the Flying Smell one expected. She's settled down now with head sunk between shoulders. Keeps looking straight skywards, perhaps at the sun as the eagle is supposed to do.... Now I seem to be having a staring match with her. ... She's gone; went suddenly with a great clatter of wings.

A later encounter occurred when the returning bird found its egg was missing from the nest.

A longish wait and the bird was back again. The female this time I thought, for there was no sign of disarranged feathers. She hurried towards the nest with her head lowered and hunched between her shoulders. She paused, slowly waddled on, reached the edge of the empty nest, and gradually sank down on it. As she lowered herself she pecked fiercely at a stick lying in the nest. Her great beak slowly sank down until it rested in the cup of the nest, touching the thin lining. She stayed like that for two minutes, perfectly still. A fly crawled unheeded over her beak. I have never seen any bird look so pathetic.

There she crouched absolutely motionless but for the blinking of her eye, unconscious of lens, hide or anything else. Of course birds show feeling; anger, joy, solicitude – you can recognise them in birds as easily as in human beings. This great vulture in front of me was only unutterably miserable. I thought, this is what a bird looks like when she returns to her nest and finds it robbed. Perhaps it sounds silly but it was a moving sight; there was something really pitiful in the bird's dumb miserable expression that I cannot describe in words, a sort of hopeless uncomprehending grappling with the calamity. One could almost see a dim clumsy intelligence trying to break through.

Griffons at the nest are an endless source of amusement and excitement. Seebohm describes the scene in *A History of British Birds* (1885).

In their breeding-habits Griffon Vultures are undoubtedly gregarious, though even then it may possibly be the nesting-sites which are gregarious rather than their occupants. They choose a perpendicular or overhanging limestone cliff in which hollows or caves rather than ledges are found at a considerable height from the ground, and generally inaccessible without a rope. They are said usually to build a great nest made of sticks, very rough on the outside, but more or less carefully smoothed and hollowed out in the middle, and lined with sheep's wool, goat's hair, dry grass, leaves, and any thing they can pick up. My Greek servant, however, assured me that he had frequently taken the eggs from a cavern where no nest was attempted; but the Greeks are such inveterate liars that I never knew when to believe him. The probable truth is, that they are not much of nest-builders, and appropriate the old nest of an Eagle or a Raven when they can. Where large nests not thus stolen are found they will most likely be the accumulated pile of many years. Both in Greece and Asia Minor I was too late for eggs, which can be obtained fresh in February and sometimes even in January; so I did not inspect many of the Griffonries very closely, though several were pointed out to me. The usual number of eggs is only one, though it is said that two are occasionally found. The stench of the Griffonries is almost insupportable. The entrance to the cavern or cleft in the rock looks as if pailfuls of whitewash had been emptied upon it; and the effluvia of ammonia and putrefaction are overpowering to all but the most enthusiastic oologist. One visit to the nest of a Vulture is sufficient to dispose for ever of the theory that these birds hunt by scent, and are endowed with highly sensitive olfactory nerves. The only condition in which the existence of animal life seems possible in a Griffonry is in the case of beings absolutely devoid of any sense of smell whatever.

In *The Birds of the British Isles* (1956), Bannerman describes a griffon colony in Spain.

In the delightful books which he wrote about Spain the late Abel Chapman has numerous references to the griffon, and in the last book he published he gives an account of the griffon colony in the great cliffs at Arcos, on the summit of which was perched the ancient Roman castle which eventually passed into his possession. The castle itself occupies the apex of the ridge, its ramparts rising from the very verge of crags 312 feet in vertical height. These crags formed – and still form – the ancestral home of a horde of huge griffon vultures whose eyries are in the caverns or on the long open ledges of the stratified limestone cliffs.

Griffon vultures – amongst the most impressive birds of all.

From a look-out post in the castle these cliffs, the vulture colony, could be kept under close observation. On winter mornings, when mist overspreads the lower land, the vultures make no attempt to set forth on the day's work before ten or even eleven o'clock, and their returning forms are to be seen again about four in the afternoon. On wet or fogbound days never a vulture quits the eyrie at all. The whole crowd sit huddled up on their ledges, for an enforced fast in no way incommodes them, used as they are to going without food for days at a stretch. On bright and sunny mornings on the contrary, all is hustle and activity, the giant birds presenting an imposing spectacle as they pass and repass along the cliff almost within reach of a stick. These morning manoeuvres may continue for half an hour or more, the vultures rising ever higher at each repeated circuit. Then for no reason all may return to the ledges, or, on the initiative of certain leaders, the whole company will strike out a bee-line in one direction or another and within brief seconds all will be lost to sight.

The return of the vultures in the evening affords another striking spectacle which Chapman describes with his inimitable pen. Between three and five o'clock, the hour depending upon visibility, the skies above the castle become punctuated with soaring forms whose varied methods of descent are delightful to watch. Some continue wheeling around with set pinions but in ever-descending circles. Others drop vertically earth-wards, the great wings just sufficiently tilted upwards and backwards, the body under perfect control. At first it appears as a mere speck, then momentarily its size increases till one realizes this speck is a vulture falling through space at amazing speed. The dive may be prolonged over 1000 feet or more, then the wings extend once again, a horizontal attitude is regained and, with a hurricane header, the vulture vanishes within its eyrie. Another and most graceful mode of descent practised by some individuals is by an interrupted spiral – dropping in a series of exact mathematical half-circles, the wing-action at each reversing point being masterly beyond words.

From being masterly beyond words, Bannerman then brings the griffon back down to earth with its more distasteful side.

If suddenly disturbed the young bird – no matter what size it may be – has a habit of instantly shamming death by throwing itself flat with its head lying in a dislocated fashion on one side; it will remain motionless for some time. Even when nearly full grown birds have been known to feign death in this extraordinary fashion. A less pleasant habit and one guaranteed to get rid of a human intruder in the minimum of time is used as a last resort – the bird recovers from its "faint" and after a series of polite bows brings up the whole of its last putrid meal. This action usually wins the day for the young vulture and the climber beats a hasty retreat before he follows the example of the bird.

Beautifully put! G. K. Yeates watched them busy on a dead horse in Andalusia (*Bird Life in Two Deltas,* undated).

April 13th. Up and about at 6 a.m. Made for the carcass at top speed.

The griffons were busy at their grisly feast. Their numbers had swollen overnight, and they were now at least forty strong. There was a pariah dog at the carcass when we arrived and the cowardly vultures were standing impatiently round watching the interloper with restless displeasure. When we approached they were very slow to leave. Most just hopped away to a safe distance. Some retired on to the rocks behind; some even perched rather precariously, on a near-by pine.

I put up a quick hide and got inside. Ten minutes sufficed to remove the scavenger's fears – or re-whet their appetites – and at last one bird risked it, and flew down close to the carcass. Immediately the fun started. Great griffons piled in from all sides, not a few alighting right on top of their fellows. They quarrelled and fought over the offal with much feeling and evil greed. An impatient bird on the fringe would make a desperate attempt to get into the middle of things by leaping on top of the seething mass and fighting his way in to the corpse. Another, successful in securing a yard or two of entrail, came charging out of the melee and played tug-o'-war with a less fortunate rival at the other end. All the time there was a continuous hissing and grunting from the scrum. A number, apparently full fed, were standing idly by, taking no part in the foul feast. A stream ran close by and often the feeding birds ran to it for a drink. I could well imagine they needed it.

In the middle of this exhibition of filthy gluttony the pariah dog came back, this time with a mate, The griffons were immediately routed. So, nearly, was I, for they chose the rocks round my hide for perches while the dogs had their say in the matter. Some were as near as five yards, perched on low boulders, and as my hide was not unlike a rock, I began to have qualms lest one would choose it for his temporary resting place. The huge birds were so close that their baleful stare seemed to cut into my very skin. I began to appreciate the agonies of having broken a leg up there in the wild sierras and to imagine that these were the loathsome scavengers come to clean me up. Ugh!

Guy Mountfort describes a similar situation in *Portrait of a Wilderness* (1958).

Provided that one has the wisdom to select a position up-wind, watching vultures feeding is an interesting if rather ghoulish experience. All vultures exhibit great caution in making the first approach to a fresh carcase, but excessive greed once the banquet has begun. The first bird to arrive circles cautiously overhead, gradually dropping lower and then examining the carcase closely from ground level or from adjacent perches on rocks or trees. Others arrive and begin waddling slowly around. Eventually one pecks tentatively at some soft part such as the eyes or belly and jumps back to see if there is any response. Once satisfied that the animal is dead, the birds begin the horrible orgy with feverish haste. Before long the carcase is smothered under a heaving, flapping, growling, hissing mob of vultures, which quickly become fouled with the viscera as they plunge their heads and shoulders inside the gaping holes torn in the body. In an incredibly short space of time nothing but the skeleton remains. Gorged with food, the vultures stagger away a few paces, temporarily incapable of flight. Other scavengers, such as the smaller vultures, carrion-eating eagles, kites, jackals and dogs, are then able to take their share.

I have several times seen the astonishing manner in which vultures discover and assemble over a carcase. The sky has been completely clear of birds when, apparently from nowhere, the first dark speck has materialized overhead. Within moments of its gradual descent other vultures have appeared from various directions and begun gliding down in converging flight. Undoubtedly vultures have magnificent long-range vision and watch each other and the smaller scavengers as they patrol the skies; a downward movement is the signal awaited and this is instantly passed on for miles around, as one after another follows suit.

The final bird of prey is another vulture which epitomises the dual character of the whole group – a magnificent bird which also becomes a foul scavenger. The Egyptian vulture can look a truly beautiful sight in a hot, sunny sky; but Meinertzhagen puts, briefly but well, the other side of the coin (*Pirates and Predators*, 1959).

One of the foulest scavengers, eating putrid offal which other vultures will not touch, even extending its beastliness to human and other excrement. On this account it has deserved the Anglo-Indian name "shawk," an abbreviation for something worse.

As a reminder of its other attributes, however, let us finish this chapter with a last extract from Bannerman's *Birds of the British Isles* (1956).

Over mountain and valley, forest and plain the Egyptian vulture will sail, ever watchful for a dying goat or mule, the feast of all others which really satisfies its wants. I have disturbed as many as forty at a carcass in

137

A Birdwatcher's Miscellany

a mountain ravine, the birds quarrelling among themselves for the choicest entrails and tearing at the flesh. When the last morsel has been picked from the hideous skeleton and the head often severed from the trunk, the overloaded vultures struggle to the nearest perch, where they will remain digesting the putrid meal, almost too lethargic to move, though at other times they will brook no close approach. Of all the vultures it has ever been my fortune to see, the Egyptian is the most loathsome feeder. Nothing foul comes amiss to it – carrion of all kinds, preferably putrid, fish entrails and offal, garbage swept up by the sea, street refuse, maggots, beetles and human excrement, which it appears to relish. I have skinned only one of these vultures in my life and the experience was not to be repeated. But, on account of the good offices which it performs, the bird is rightly protected almost wherever it is found.

How different does the Egyptian vulture appear in one's eyes when seen in its immaculate white plumage with black primaries widely extended, soaring against a cloudless blue sky. Watch it steadily mounting to the heavens, tilting now one wing, now the other, to catch the air currents, and with each widening circle growing smaller and smaller until the tiny speck is lost in space. It is difficult then to remember how repellent it can be at close quarters, when the bare yellow neck and forehead give it an almost obscene appearance.

The extracts in this chapter illustrate the two sides to all birds of prey: their beauty and, often, sheer magnificence, and their less pleasant predatory and scavenging activities. Even keen birdwatchers sometimes find them unacceptable. Others think they are the most exciting of all. Certainly anything which helps to spread an appreciation and understanding of the essential role they play in the natural world must be very welcome.

4 WILDFOWL

Most people like ducks. Their association with park ponds and ornamental collections goes against them in some birdwatchers' minds, but is a bonus point for others. Feral geese seem, to some, to devalue the group when the local gravel pit holds a motley mixture of semi-tame birds in the summer, but there is never any denying the real excitement and adventure which true wild geese can provide in their winter retreats. Where better to start this chapter than with Sir Peter Scott, founder of the Wildfowl Trust. In *The Eye of the Wind* (1977) he recalled his early discovery of Slimbridge.

In the autumn of 1945 I received two letters from ornithologist friends which, taken in conjunction, were to have a very profound effect on my life. Both these letters were from farmers and both concerned wild geese. The first was from Howard Davis, an experienced observer of birds living near Bristol, who sent me a copy of a paper he had written on the great flock of White-fronted Geese which has wintered on the Severn Estuary from immemorial times. If I could spare the time to come down, he wrote, he would like to show them to me. I remembered my brief visit there before the war, at a time when the main flock had just left on the spring migration. I had seen, as I recalled, a bunch of twenty or thirty and that was all, and I had examined with interest the old duck decoy in the little wood. It would be nice to go there again, but I wondered when, if ever, there would be time.

The second letter was from my old and valued farmer friend Will Tinsley. At the beginning of the war some of the best birds from my lighthouse collection had been taken over to his farm to live happily in the orchard and about the farmyard. Among these had been a pair of Lesser White-fronted Geese, perhaps the most beautiful of all the world's grey geese which I had first met in Hungary and later in their thousands on the Caspian shore.

At that time the Lesser Whitefront was the rarest British bird; it had only been recorded once, and on any list you cannot have a rarer bird than that. It shared that distinction with some twenty other species which had only been recorded once in Britain. This single record was in 1886 when an immature Lesser Whitefront was shot in Northumberland by Alfred Crawhal Chapman, brother of Abel Chapman, the famous wildfowler and author. The Lesser White-fronted Goose breeds as far west as Scandinavia and from there eastwards across sub-arctic Europe and Asia almost to the Pacific. Those Lesser Whitefronts which breed in Lapland fly south-eastwards on their winter migrations, through Hungary to Macedonia and the Mediterranean.

I had brought some slightly wounded Kis Lilliks (the first word, pronounced Kish, meaning small) back with me from the plains of the Hortobágy to my lighthouse home. When the war came and my collection of live waterfowl was disbanded, a pair of Kis Lilliks was taken over to join Will Tinsley's collection of geese which lived in the orchard beside his house. Now in his letter Will reported an extraordinary occurrence; he said that in 1943 a wild Lesser White-fronted Goose had come down one day out of the sky and landed beside his tame pair and had stayed there for several days. There was little chance that the bird could have escaped from any other collection, but as a truly wild bird it was only the second which had been so far recorded in Britain. I had no doubt whatever about the identification. I remember saying to myself, "If Will says it was a Lesser, then a Lesser it most certainly was." From this I fell to wondering how many people there were in this country who would know the difference between a Lesser Whitefront and an ordinary Whitefront.

It is, to be sure, a little smaller but not much; its bill is a good deal smaller and rather pinker, but the only definite distinguishing character is the golden yellow eyelid which encircles the eye of the Lesser Whitefront. How often, in the field, can a wild goose's eyelids be critically examined? Supposing, I thought, these Lesser White-fronts came regularly to the British Isles, who would recognise them? Of course, Will Tinsley would, but I could not think of very many others. And if they came, where should one look for them? It seemed to me that

A lesser white-fronted goose grazing with white-fronts.

they would be most likely to mix accidentally with those species of geese which migrated to Britain from breeding grounds further to the east. Two species of grey geese do this – the Bean Goose and the Common or Russian Whitefront, and the largest flock of Russian Whitefronts in Britain in winter was to be found on the Severn Estuary. Here, then, was the chance of putting my theory to the test. If it was correct I might expect to find a stray Lesser Whitefront among the larger geese if I could only get close enough to see their eyelids.

A few weeks later I was staying in Stafford and suggested to my friends John Winter and Clive Wilson that we might take up Howard Davis's invitation; on the following day, after a telephone arrangement, we met him at Slimbridge. We walked from the bridge over the canal and down to the end of the lane, after which he led us out towards a war-time pillbox commanding a view of the saltings upon which the geese were feeding. Bent double, we crept across the field, behind the low sea-wall and into the dank concrete box. From the embrasures we had a most wonderful view of a great flock of 2000 wild geese. Among them we saw, quite near-by, a young Bean Goose, then a Barnacle, and a Brent and later a Greylag. There were also a few Pinkfeet but the majority were, as they should have been, Russian-bred Whitefronts. That evening we went back to stay with Howard Davis at his farm near Bristol. As he drove me back in his car I outlined my wild idea about the Lesser Whitefronts and was rash enough to suggest that it was for this very purpose that we had come down to the Severn. On the following day we were back in the pillbox again overlooking the green Dumbles and the grey carpet of wild geese. Again the young Bean Goose was close in front of us.

We had been in the pillbox, I suppose, for a little over half an hour when Howard Davis said quietly, "There's a bird here which interests me. Would you have a look at it?" In a few moments he had directed me to the goose in question among the tight mass of geese in front of us, and the instant my binoculars lit upon it I realised that it was a Lesser Whitefront. My spine tingled delightfully as it does in the slow movement of Sibelius's Violin Concerto. Here almost too easily was a vindication of my far-fetched theory. It was, no doubt, a small recondite discovery, a minor ornithological technicality, yet for me it was a moment of unforgettable exultation – a major triumph, an epoch-making occurrence, a turning point; or is it only in looking back on it that I have invested it with so much significance because, in the event, it changed the course of my life?

From the pillbox we watched the little Lesser Whitefront for half an hour or more, satisfying ourselves that the eyelids were in fact golden yellow, that the bill was small and extra-pink, and that the white forehead patch rose high on to the crown of the head. The bird had that smooth, dark, perfect look, almost as if there was a bloom on the feathers, which is so characteristic of the Lesser Whitefront.

Later in the afternoon we moved further down the sea-wall to get a better view of a part of the flock which was beyond the fence that crosses the Dumbles at the half-way mark. Here among 200 or 300 more Whitefronts was a second Lesser Whitefront. To make certain, we went back and found our original bird still almost in the position in which we had left it. Here then undoubtedly were two Lesser Whitefronts; if Will Tinsley's war-time bird was to be accepted, as I felt sure it should be, these were the third and fourth specimens of their kind ever to be authentically recorded in Britain. It is not often that one sees so rare a British bird and it may be imagined with what excitement we telephoned that evening to a number of ornithological pundits. The meticulous and eversceptical Bernard Tucker after much cross-questioning professed himself convinced, but I was privately glad that he saw them for himself a week later. In the following year we saw three Lesser Whitefronts and in most of the succeeding years in this Severn flock there have been at least one, sometimes as many as six of them, appearing as strays among the Russian White-fronted Geese.

On that sunny day in December 1945 the third and fourth Lesser Whitefronts had brought the total number of kinds of wild geese we had seen together on that marsh to seven, and as we walked back from the pillbox I came to the inescapable conclusion that this was the place in which anyone who loved wild geese must live. Here were two empty cottages which might become the headquarters of the research organisation which had been taking shape in my mind over the war years, the headquarters of a new collection of waterfowl, of the scientific and educational effort which I believed was so badly needed for the conservation of wildfowl. As we squelched up the track, past the 100-year-old duck decoy, into the deep-rutted yard and back along the muddy lane towards the canal, I looked at my surroundings with a new eye, an eye to the future, for this was the beginning of the Wildfowl Trust.

In *Birds of the Grey Wind* (1940) the Reverend E. A. Armstrong writes of brent geese at Strangford Lough.

Wonderful as are the multitudes of waders and ducks it is the tribe of the wild geese – grey spirits riding so masterfully the grey wind – which are the especial glory of the lough in winter. Brents are easily the most abundant on Strangford; the other species are comparatively meagrely represented. Grey lags are seen occasionally and it is believed that this is the goose which old writers describe as breeding on a bog in County Down in the eighteenth century. A shooting friend once described to me his bewilderment when a number of apparently tame geese near a farm-house suddenly took wing. They were wild grey lags. For a moment he felt as much amazed as if a flock of turkeys had soared into the sky. But these geese favour the Downpatrick marshes rather than the bare flats.

The Strangford brents often spend the night in the southern reaches of the lough. They come up to the northern shores in the mornings to feed if the mud banks are uncovered. What a sight it is as they advance! – flying in wide-spreading arcs or chevrons, skein after skein, coming into view as long lines of tiny specks high above the water and swerving grandly as they come down to the slob land. As the smaller gaggles draw near, their resonant travel-talk is heard, a virile '*onk, onk, orrok, orrok*'; but when large flocks are resting on the water this busy chatter reaches the fascinated listener as a hoarse continuous clamour, rising and falling like the tumult from a vast encampment. One might believe the geese to be a communistic army in which every private is entitled to express his opinion of the plan of campaign! But I have watched a pair for two hours at twenty-five yards range and heard no sound from them until they flew away. Some writers have compared the cry of a flock of brent geese to the music of hounds, while others have questioned the accuracy of this comparison. Thompson, replying in *Birds of Ireland* to such critics, retorted that his hunter responded to the music of the geese as to the baying of hounds. The fact is that the sound varies according to the size and distance of the flocks. Incidentally, how similar is the uproar from the party of spawning frogs to the distant clamour of a skein of grey geese!

Many pale-bellied brent geese winter in Ireland.

When they alight, the birds stand looking about them for a time before beginning to feed, preen, and bathe. With bent necks they gobble the slitch grass, following the receding tide, or walking before it if it is rising; sometimes, like swans, they may up-end in the shallow water and stretch down to the mud, showing their white sterns. They prefer to feed on the mud flats, for they can devour the *Zostera* much more expeditiously when they are not afloat. As they swim, long festoons of the weed often hang from their bills. Their normal swimming speed when not feeding is remarkably fast. As a rule they feed by day, though the state of the tide may force them to come to the mud flats at dusk. Now and then a small pack does not go out to safety in deep water during the day. I have surprised them at midday resting on the grassy margins of the islands and there is no doubt that occasionally they will feed on grass like their grey brethren. They tend to graze when the slitch grass is scarce.

One of my most vivid memories of the lough is the sight of a gaggle of geese flying past in the light of the setting sun. I was standing on the crest of an island when the geese came speeding by, not seventy yards distant, grunting and croaking. The light shone full upon them as they passed in powerful flight – black outstretched necks adorned with little collars, grey, vermiculated backs contrasting with silver bellies, the dark wings of the phalanx beating a common measure but not in time. It is this mingled regularity and irregularity which is the secret, I suspect, of the satisfying artistic pattern which they present. So they passed against a background of watery blue sky and fields as green as only Irish fields can be in winter.

The morning flight on a winter's dawn on the north-east coast of England was described by Abel Chapman, in *Bird Life of the Borders* (1907).

As the first streak of dawn becomes discernible in the eastern skies – or rather a trifle before that period – there commences a general movement of wildfowl, and from a favourable position (usually near the mouth of the seaward channel) the whole local stock of fowl may be observed in the course of an hour or two's watching – the night-feeding birds speeding outwards to the open sea, and those of diurnal habit hurrying in, hungry, to their feeding-grounds within the harbour.

At first it is pitch dark, the rude features of the coast scenery but dimly discernible, and only the wild cry of some seafowl blends with the roar of the breakers outside. First to move are the mallards, then the wigeon; both of these, in winter, go out to sea before a symptom of daylight has appeared. They are only recognisable by their well-known notes (if uttered), or by the resonant swish, swish of their strong pinions, distinctly audible far up in the dark skies. Perhaps the stately lines of the mallards may be discerned for a moment against some cloud-bank – wigeon never form line, but hurry out in confused mass. Next to these come the mergansers, the first of the "inward-bound" from the sea. They come singly, or in twos and threes, flying very close, as though linked together, and at tremendous speed. Then the darkness resounds with the vibrations of a thousand wings, as a shapeless mass of godwits or knots rush past from inside, or a string of oystercatchers pass overhead – all these waders being driven out as the sand-banks disappear under the flowing tide. The latter bear a strong resemblance to duck as they file out in line on drooping pinion, and in the uncertain light many a "sea-pyot" has lost his life, owing to this unfortunate similitude to his superiors. The waders are not, of course, bound for the sea, but for some extensive salt-marsh or sandflats they wot of alongshore, where they can rest in security during high water.

As the light gradually strengthens towards the dawn, spectral forms

Grey geese provide some of the most spectacular birdwatching in Europe.

loom silently overhead; these are the big gulls diligently searching the waters for their breakfast, and the boisterous laughter of the small black-headed gull resounds from the tideway beyond the bar. Early one January morning a glaucous gull settled down on the water close at hand, carried off one dead godwit, and deliberately pulled another to bits.

Next a grebe may come spinning along. Close to the water he flies, and, considering the shortness of his wings, at amazing speed. Then a few golden-eyes, usually singly, and always very high, pass inwards. Meanwhile the geese are on the move; and, in the dim light seawards, one descries, far away over the dark waters, what might be the edge of a little cloud, or the smoke of a distant steamer, as they go through their matutinal evolutions preparatory to "coming inside." For some ten minutes these evolutions continue, and in the increasing light the forms of their dense columns become gradually discernible, gyrating rapidly to and fro beyond the line of breakers to seaward. Presently, rank, after rank, they head up for the harbour, always high in air, unless half a gale blows right in their teeth, and pass up the channel, clanging down, as it were, a glorious defiance to man to do his worst. As daylight becomes fully established, there appear the weird-looking divers (*Colymbi*) usually the last, or perhaps an unwieldy cormorant brings up the rear; and now the rim of the sun appears above the eastern horizon, and one lingers a few minutes longer while the eye revels in the gorgeous hues and lovely effects of a sunrise over the sea.

The Canon C. E. Raven (*Bird Haunts and Bird Behaviour*, 1929) evoked the wonderful appeal of the south coast marshes in 1929 – still a problem to put over to potential 'developers' who can see no value in such places.

When you leave the little red town, sleeping in a warm glow upon its hill, and cross the bridge where artists bring their easels of an evening and golfers hustle off to catch the tram, you plunge into a strange world. Far away to the north a line of blue downs fades into the sky: to the south the flat seems to stretch to the end of the world: here and there the tower of a church, the roof of a barn, or a clump of wind swept trees breaks the line of its expanse: the reed-filled ditches and low embankments merely increase the sense of infinite space. To come from the hedgerows and coppices, the up and down of the home counties to this featureless immensity is like plunging from the delta of the Nile into the Libyan desert.

The marsh is famous for its sheep and for its birds. Tramping home at midnight from a round of mothing in the sandhills I have listened to the queer cries of the Moorhens, always restless in the darkness, and been startled by the rush of a Mallard flushed from a dyke. As I stole down in a grey September dawn to watch the migrants on the beach, a Heron would loom up monstrously large from his fishing and fade into the twilight on slow-moving wings. By day wave upon wave of birds would halt for twenty-four hours in the pasture; today every anthill is bright with Yellow Wagtails: yesterday the railings were crowded with Whinchats: tomorrow Pipits will be fluttering from field to field.

A. W. Boyd (*The Country Diary of a Cheshire Man*, 1946) included many encounters with wildfowl in his book. Bewick's swans obviously impressed him.

January 7th, 1943

As I stood to-day in a little wood by the mere I heard a high-pitched melodious yelping as if from a pack of aerial hounds. Through the trees I watched a flight of Bewick's swans drop down out of the sky, circle round, and settle in the middle of the mere for a brief time, but long enough to let me examine them through my telescope and see that they included two young ones with dusky plumage. They soon rose again, and the yelping increased as they were joined by a little group that had been hidden from sight behind the reeds. Twenty-seven in all, they flew in a long line at a great height and soon passed from sight towards the western estuaries. They rose lightly from the water, with none of the laborious clatter of semi-tame mute swans, five of which were still swimming there with stately unconcern after the smaller wild swans had gone. This winter seems destined to be marked by the appearance of unusual numbers of these swans, which occur only irregularly in Cheshire and rarely in large numbers.

The effects of weather on wildfowl and their habitat were often detailed by Boyd.

January 30th, 1930

There is one Cheshire mere that rarely freezes; when the others are covered with skaters Rostherne is often untouched by ice, and not since 1895 has it been completely frozen. Though the thaw had come, ice still covered most of the meres, but a visit to this unfrozen one showed that not all the waterfowl had left our inhospitable countryside for the estuaries and the coast. Mallard and teal were much more abundant than all other duck together – I estimated that there were fully two thousand – and, as if to show their appreciation of this sanctuary, the drake teal were displaying in their own peculiar way. The presence of a duck to egg them on did not seem to be needed; a bunch of drakes found in the presence of one another all the stimulus they required. They darted at each other, and first one and then a second would throw his head forward and then backwards with a jerk, following this by pointing his tail straight up (as if to show off the yellow triangular patches) and then plunging forward. It was a strange performance and several groups were showing their exuberance in this way.

STAFFORDSHIRE. *December 31st, 1937*

I saw a goosander at the end of November, although this duck seldom appears here till the New Year. Two days after Christmas I was again passing the Staffordshire pool where I had seen the first. The fog and mist, which at least lent approval to the belief that Christmas should be spent at home, had lifted, and it was possible to see half-way across the water. The first thing that came into view was a long line of goosanders – thirty-nine of them; of these only six were drakes in full plumage, but these six were full of spirit, and with repeated dashes at one another were playing the goosanders' version of the game of "tig."

Many of the commoner wildfowl are worthy of study. Henry Seebohm wrote about tufted ducks in *A History of British Birds* (1885).

My first acquaintance with the Tufted Duck was made in this district five-and-twenty years ago at Clumber; and more recently I have been indebted to the kindness of my friend Mr Whitaker, of Rainworth Lodge (within twenty yards of which they breed), for an opportunity of examining their habits more closely. One of the tributaries of the Idle river rises in a large wood on the Newstead estate, and flows through a succession of little lakes, ponds, and swamps, where the Tufted Duck may be seen all the year round. Mr Whitaker estimates the number of pairs breeding in this district at more than a hundred. It is not an uncommon thing to see five or six pairs on each pond besides Mallard and Shoveller, numerous Waterhens and Coots, and a few Grebes. The Tufted Duck pairs in March, and is seen in pairs until early in June, when the female begins to sit. At this season the male is devotedly attached to her, and the pair are always seen together. They are not very wild, and may be approached with care within a comparatively short distance. The male is the first to show any alarm, and sometimes swims backwards and forwards, showing his anxiety to his more stolid mate, but never venturing to take wing until she has risen from the water, and then following her to the next pond, or in her circuitous course up to the head of the water, when she will often wheel round, and passing behind any cover that may happen to be on the side of the pond, drop down again with her faithful attendant not far from the spot where she was originally disturbed. During the daytime they are very quiet, floating on the water near the middle of the pond, sometimes sleeping with their heads under their wings, and occasionally lazily preening their feathers. When at rest the male is very conspicuous, and seems to float very light on the water, his white breast-feathers fluffed up over his wings so as almost to hide them. Sometimes as he leans over on the side away from the observer he looks quite white, and then as he rolls back again to preen the other side he suddenly changes into black. When his head is erect, the black crest is easily seen. Towards evening they begin to feed. Exactly as twilight marks the approach of night, they rise from the pond where they have spent the day, and fly up stream to other ponds to feed, returning in the morning; Whitaker says, "flying at a great pace and a good height in the air. In the morning, after their return to the ponds, they may be seen actively diving for weeds, usually remaining under water about fifteen seconds, and resorting to the middle of the pond. In the afternoon they rest or may be seen preening their feathers, but towards flight-time they become restless, frequently calling and taking short flights until the time arrives to go, when with loud cries they rise together, and rush on swift pinions to their breeding-places."

The smart, black-and-white tufted duck.

Walpole-Bond (*Field Studies of some Rarer British Birds*, 1914) gives a fine description of gadwalls in their breeding sites.

Early morning is the surest time to observe the Gadwall, when the birds – like ourselves – are enjoying the freshness of a Norfolk spring dawn. Then they are up and stirring, flying, generally in pairs or small lots, in wide, vagrant circles, now over the "brecks" and any coverts adjoining the stream, now above the stream itself and its wooded quagmires. Generally at an easy elevation, they sometimes ascend to a good height, when (there would, perhaps, be four or five together) high revelry may be held. At first one chases another. Then the tables are turned; pursuer becomes pursued. Then all take the air. A certain pitch is reached, and down they all come again, still on the slant, and often diving about curiously, aerial tactics which, with slight modifications, are common to most ducks during the breeding-season. At another time, as a pair

HB.

Gadwalls are subtle, unobtrusive ducks.

flash over a patch of water, a third Gadwall – a drake, who certainly has a sitting duck not very far away – rises dripping from the pool and buffets the intruding drake of the pair smartly. Periodically, tiring of their aerial play, they will descend waterwards, each pair to its respective domain, pitching with infinite ease; and mid-stream, or at any rate a spot well removed from prospective danger, is vastly preferred to the margin of the water. Occasionally one will seek the sandy patches of soil chess-boarding the heath-covered waste adjacent, where one might suppose the ducks would nest (and especially in a wet season), instead of, and as they nearly always do, close to the river bank, where they are often flooded out.

The Gadwall's garb, if sober, is pleasing, but there is nothing specially attractive in its appearance, for the drake's upper-parts, excepting the rump, which is glossy black, are washed with black and whitish bars on an otherwise brown surface. The under neck-feathers and breast are a mixture of sootiness and white, which, as the bird flies overhead, creates a uniform dark appearance. The rest of the under-parts, however, are like étiolated sateen. His wings alone deserve high commendation; on them you will admire a bold pattern of black, white, and chestnut. The duck has a plumage of brown with creamy-buff markings, and shows no black on the upper tail-coverts. Her throat and neck incline to fulvous, and below she is not so conspicuously bleached, but – apart from the chestnut – she enjoys the same wing-decoration. This description of the plumage, however, must be taken as that seen through binoculars – a sort of bird's eye view, so to say.

E. A. Armstrong devoted a whole chapter of *Birds of the Grey Wind* (1940) to 'the magnificent merganser' – and who is to say that a drake red-breasted merganser in perfect plumage does not deserve such a description?

If beautiful plumes together with peculiar and interesting behaviour constitute the bird-lover's criteria of that which gives greatest delight he should cultivate the acquaintance of the red-breasted merganser. This gorgeous bird has never received the appreciation he deserves. Thousands of poets, artists, and writers have lavished praise on the kingfisher, yet hardly a voice has been raised in honour of the merganser. The very name is clumsy, ugly, and repellent. The kingfisher is a fine fellow, of course, but if the truth must be told, he is also a trifle vulgar, for dazzling and exotic apparel do not make a gentleman. He is somewhat inclined to be corpulent, flies rather ponderously, conducts his courtship in the crudest way by hunting his beloved along the steam, and soils his nest as foully as a hoopoe. Even if the measure of our esteem be merely splendour of appearance the merganser surpasses the kingfisher, for he is comely in form as well as bright in plumage. It is a strange thing that both these ardent fishermen should be endowed with ruddy breasts, burnished plumage, and red feet, and that the insect-, seed-, and flesh-eaters should come off so badly in comparison with them. The kingfisher and the merganser have a good claim to be our two brightest birds, for such gaudy fry as bee-eaters, hoopoes, and orioles must be considered adventurous vagrants rather than true natives. They have never quite taken to us – more's the pity. The merganser is a true native of the bleak hyperborean regions. Its extensive breeding range includes the northerly parts of Europe, Asia, and North America, and as a European nesting bird it comes farthest south in Ireland, if we except the occasional clutches recorded from time to time in Holland. In England the merganser is only known as a bird of passage, appearing along the coast and on inland reservoirs out of the breeding season. In Scotland it breeds and is said to be increasing; and in Ireland, too, it has recently extended its range. On such waters as Strangford Lough it is common. The shallow shores of this miniature Mediterranean offer productive hunting, and its islands provide congenial seclusion for the nesting birds. Pairs also breed, now and then, on some of the islets in the open sea off the Antrim coast.

Many a time have I watched the courtship antics of the saw-bills, as these birds are called in Ulster, but I confess that the precise meaning of it all is still beyond my comprehension. Creep with me through the alder thickets which fringe Lough Neagh's shore, down where the Lodden Lily dangles giant snowdrops above thick tufts of daffodilly leaves; and let us hide behind the regimented bayonets of the irises guarding the water-side. Presently there is a swish of strongly beating pinions overhead and a bunch of these ducks swerves past and settles in

Red-breasted mergansers – striking in pattern and delicate in form.

a shallow lagoon. Immediately all is turmoil and excitement. There is a mighty splashing and flogging of the water as the birds dash at each other, a constant coming and going, fluttering and plunging. An aquatic tournament is in progress and the lists are thronged with gay and ardent paladins parading their splendour, threatening, bragging, and jousting, seemingly beside themselves with excitement. This scene of frantic activity contrasts strangely with the placid lough, a silver mirror to the contemplative trees and tranquil sky.

The most extraordinary aspect of the performance has yet to be described. As the birds career back and forth they constantly open wide their slender, serrated, red bills. They bob quickly and then shoot up head and neck into the air, gaping widely. It looks almost as if the birds were having spasms or retching uncontrollably towards the heavens. The females, too, will occasionally stretch up their necks, perform a sudden, wide yawn and bring their heads down with a quick pump-handle motion. Grace and pride of beauty are set aside, and the agitated birds jerk and belch with what seems to the spectator painful vigour and intensity. "A mad world, my masters," one might be inclined to say on first seeing this ludicrous pantomime amidst the still beauty of the Irish springtide.

Courtship procedure proper varies to a very considerable degree but in its more elaborate phases follows more or less this formula: The drake swims up to the duck, who appears quite unconcerned. He approaches with red beak raised at an angle of about seventy-five degrees and slender neck held in line like an ancient ship's "beak"; and as he comes up with the lady he performs a sudden bow, uttering at the same time a low purring or scraping note. As he bobs, the wings are slightly arched upwards, displaying the black-barred white secondaries, and the tail is elevated and, sometimes, spread. It should be noted that the stretching upwards of the neck exhibits the white collar to fullest advantage. Rising in the water to show off his breast-band he dips again, and now with his tufted crest fully erected and head twisted at an angle of some sixty degrees to the water, but towards the female, he opens his bill to its fullest extent, as in a gigantic yawn, revealing to her its brilliant red interior. After watching this spectacle the philosophic observer is apt to reflect that the ways of birds in love are no less strange than those of men.

Collingwood Ingram (*In Search of Birds,* 1966) described eiders, including their chicks.

In one corner of the sanctuary, not far from the sea, there existed a scattered colony of Eider Ducks. The birds made little or no attempt to conceal their nests and, even when one of these might have conceivably escaped notice, the female usually drew one's attention to it by blundering clumsily off her eggs. At the time of my visits (which on both occasions were in the latter half of June) their eggs were mostly in an advanced state of incubation while not a few had already hatched. From one nest the mother had evidently taken her family to the sea without waiting to complete her brood for a single egg had been left abandoned in the nest which, I discovered, contained a dead chick.

This gave me an excellent opportunity to make a careful study of a fully developed embryo of this duck – an opportunity that enabled me to make a very interesting discovery. I found on examination that its body was covered with what appeared at first sight to be a coating of coarse damp hair. A closer scrutiny, however, revealed that this was in fact down and that its hair-like appearance was solely due to each individual feather being tightly encased in a long tubular-shaped sheath – a provision of nature obviously devised to protect the feather's delicate structure from being wetted or damaged by the slimy moisture which is always present in an egg immediately before hatching. After the chick has emerged from the shell, and almost as soon as it has become dry (a process quickly effected by the warmth of the brooding mother's body),

The female eider settles onto her nest, lined with her own down.

these enveloping sheaths, or protective coverings, start to disintegrate from the base upwards, and in a surprisingly short time the baby Eider is transformed from a damp bedraggled-looking object into a charming little duckling of familiar aspect – a small fluffy creature clothed in down of a blackish colour. Although proof is lacking, it is probable that the down feathers on the embryos of all the duck family are similarly protected, and this may be true also of the young of other species whose nestlings are born with a downy covering.

Like waders, some wildfowl add to their appeal by breeding in remote northern wildernesses. Seebohm watched pintails in Siberia (*A History of British Birds*, 1885) in the days when shooting birds was still an acceptable practice for a birdwatcher!

When Harvie-Brown and I were at Ust Zylma, on the banks of the Petchora, waiting for summer to come, we saw one of the most interesting episodes in the history of migration that I have ever witnessed. The river Zylma enters the Petchora opposite the village, and when the melting of the snow in the valley of the Upper Petchora causes the great river to rise, its waters flow up the little stream, which overflows its banks, floods the low-lying meadows in many places, and forms little lakes and small fjords or *couriers* of open water a week or more before the ice breaks up. The Sessedatel of Ust Zylma, Mons. Znaminski (one of the few Russian officials who deserves the honourable title of gentleman, and who has since, I am happy to hear, been promoted to be Ispravnik of Ust Ishma), had a shooting-box some miles up the river, and invited us to join him and the Postmaster in an

155

expedition to shoot *outka* or Ducks. On the 19th of May we hired a sledge and joined our host and his friend, crossed the great river (a mile and a half) over the snow on the ice, and reached the wooden house after some adventures among the melting snow-fields. Early the next morning the sight that presented itself to our view was a most interesting one. As far as we could see, the strip of open water on each side of the ice in the Zylma was black with Ducks, and overhead Ducks were flying about in every direction like a swarm of bees. To estimate the number at half a million would probably be to guess under the mark. They were almost all of them Pintails, but many Teal and Wigeon were among them. In spite of their enormous numbers they were wild enough. We had no difficulty in watching them through our glasses so as to identify the species; but when it came to getting within shot, we found the only way was to conceal ourselves behind a willow-stump and take them as they flew over. After the weary waiting for summer to come, with comparatively few birds to watch except the flocks of Snow-Buntings, Shore-Larks, and Lapland Buntings, it was most exciting to find ourselves in the midst of such abundance of bird-life; nor was the prospect of unlimited roast duck by any means to be despised after a month's diet of salt beef. We did not, however, enjoy it long on this occasion, for on the morning of the next day we were startled to find that our road on the ice of the Zylma had broken up into pack-ice, and was steadily marching down to the Petchora. We were obliged to desert our baggage, and, after a forced march to the mouth of the river, were fortunate enough to find a boat waiting for us, which, thanks to the important position of our host, had been sent across the ice to our rescue. As we crossed the ice we could hear it cracking like thunder under our feet; and the next morning we found that the ice on the great river had broken up, and we were effectually cut off from our baggage and the Pintails by a mass of rapidly drifting pack-ice, which continued to march past for five days.

The appeal of wildfowl seems for many birdwatchers to lie in the wonderful spectacle of the moving flocks against a dawn sky or emerging ghost-like through an autumn mist. The sheer numbers as well as the graceful flight of these birds can take the breath away. Individually they are colourful and fascinating. It is surely of the utmost importance that we preserve the wetlands and marshes which form their habitat so that we can continue to enjoy them in their natural state. This is a theme which is explored more fully in the beginning of the next chapter.

5 WADERS AND WILDERNESS

There can hardly be a birdwatcher who does not claim to be a wader enthusiast. Birds of prey are not everyone's cup of tea; little drab warblers may excite some with their problems of identification but put others off for just that reason; wildfowl are an obsession for some, but neglected by others. Waders seem to achieve just the balance which allows everyone to appreciate them – their beauty of plumage and elegance of form, the purity of their songs and calls, the evocative places in which they live, their enormous globe-trotting journeys, in many cases the difficulty of identification (and always the likelihood of something unusual turning up almost anywhere). Altogether, they make a favourite and fascinating group. Much of their fascination comes from the fact that they are long-distance migrants which may be familiar out of the breeding season (even abundant) but which go far away to the north to breed in unexplored regions of the Siberian tundra, or perhaps remote valleys of Greenland.

G. K. Yeates, in *A Bird Lover's Britain* (1937) describes the more familiar birds: those which breed in accessible parts of Britain. With drainage already having accounted for the destruction of most wet areas of lowland Britain, and an ever-present threat to those which remain, it is as well to be reminded of the attractions of an old-fashioned marsh.

To the uninitiated, marshland spells a dreary, flat, uninteresting landscape from which scenery, in the conventional meaning of the

A bunch of lapwings.

word, is conspicuously absent. A sluggish, winding river, with the bushy-topped pollard willows dancing attendance upon its banks, and straight-cut, reed-fringed dikes which drain the valley, would seem to offer little attraction.

Yet upon those who know their spirit and have come to love it, the marshes exert a fascination which not even the great hills of the north can rival. To one who knows them, both on hot June days when the reed and sedge warblers make their incessant music, and again in winter when floods drown the meadows that in summer harbour redshank and lapwing, the marshes bring a feeling of airy well-being. For depression and despondency there is no better tonic, for who could fail to be invigorated by their spaciousness? Indeed it is this openness of theirs, this feeling of freedom they inspire, which is the centre-point of the fascination of marshland. Wide and often entirely uncultivated, they inspire the human mind by their wide uninterrupted horizons, in which the scattered, gnarled old willows stand gauntly silhouetted against the sky behind. And in summer, through the brilliance of their kingcups, the luxuriance of their growth, the cattle browsing contentedly and the strange noises that issue forth from the reeds they have a charm to which even the biggest dullard cannot surely be wholly blind.

Whatever the feelings, however, which they may raise in him, the bird lover cannot afford to neglect the marshes and water meadows, for they harbour a type of bird life which is only to be seen at its best in such an environment. The dense reed-beds and long grass can provide many exciting moments as those who have once seen a harrier hunting will know well enough; while amongst the smaller birds a discriminating eye may pick out, in the right localities, from amongst the myriads of yellow wagtails, a pair of the rare blue-headed form. And at migration time, when birds are passing through, where is there more likely a place to find the unexpected? Indeed, it is the surprises of marshland birding that make it so attractive. The withy-bed, the reed-fringed pool, and the muddy corner of the winding river – from all and any comes the chance of something unexpected and something new. Not that it must be assumed that the study of birds necessarily centres round the chronicling and recording of the unusual and the rare. Just as much attention must be paid to the everyday species. Yet he is a strange man who does not find in the occurrence of the occasional rarity an added spice to his daily rounds.

The lapwing is one of the birds which are essential features of the English countryside. Yet his haunts are widespread, and he is as readily found on the hills and downlands as on the wetter ground in the valleys beneath. In one and all he fits his environment, and in none is he more at home than in the water meadow – or so it seems to me, and all of us must have our own personal impressions of the typical country we associate with each species of bird.

Side by side with the lapwing in the marshland country we associate the redshank and snipe. In fact, if anything, the melodious whistling call of the one and the sharp-sounding "drumming" of the other are even more typical of the water meadows than the lapwing's attractive pee-wit.

John Day, in the recent book *RSPB Nature Reserves* (1983), details the importance of the remaining wet meadows of an increasingly dried-out Britain.

On its way to the sea, the river leaves the urgency of the hills and moves in a more leisurely fashion, swaying through winding channels across the flat hinterlands. There, after the rains, the swollen waters slowly overtop the banks and quietly spead across the flat meadows, depositing their rich silts and invigorating the herb-rich natural turf. For centuries man has lived with this natural rhythm, grazing his herds and cutting hay amongst the rich flush of summer grass and leaving the wet, winter swards to the fishermen, wildfowlers, eelcatchers, and, of course, the birds. In some places the natural waterways were harnessed and, using sophisticated sluice systems and channels, the meadows could be flooded artificially after the first hay cut or early bite. Later, the rejuvenated fields were drained, enabling a second crop to be gathered.

These were the managed water meadows, now largely gone, the artistry of their cycles forgotten.

Over the years, man has constantly sought to improve on this natural system, rivers have been canalised, their banks raised and the meadows ditched and pumped. By maintaining lower, and constant, water tables, it was possible to plough up the old turf with its rich mixture of water-loving herbs and grasses, and plant the improved ryegrass mixtures, without fear of winter floods.

Improved drainage with field drains supplementing the ditches, allowed crops to be grown over thousands of acres. With the advent of modern electric pumps in the 1930s and 1940s this process was speeded up. Corn, barley and potatoes flourished in the reclaimed meadowland and the birds, their numbers sadly reduced by the effect of earlier drainage and improvement, were finally forced to leave for good. But in a few, a very few places, this process has not reached finality, and the traditional farming patterns are still followed. West Sedgemoor is such a place.

For many people the true character of an old wet grassland site like this is most evident in the spring, when the startling green washlands have emerged from their winter covering of floodwater and stretch like an emerald sword, cutting through the monotonous brown fens, where the spring wheat is just beginning to cover the dark soils in a thin, blue-green film. The winter wildfowl have gone. Huge flocks of noisy, self-confident wigeon, the graceful pintail and swift flights of teal have left. Gone too are the wild swans – whoopers and Bewick's – which until a few weeks ago could be seen in unhurried family groups, breasting the brown floodwaters or flighting over the wash banks. Nearly seven months will pass before they return from their breeding grounds in the northern wastes. The resident ducks are left behind; mallard and shoveler, gadwall, teal and tufted duck, now in pairs along the ditches or by the receding flashes of water.

Some birds are already making their nests in the long grass tussocks, and will soon be launching their ducklings on the quiet waters of the rivers and dykes. The air is full of sound. Larks are singing, high above the bank, their song interrupted by the drumming of a snipe, as the bird knifes through the sky with a sound like tearing cloth. Below, the redshank call from the gatepost tops and the nuptial "wicka-wicka" of black-tailed godwits carries across the river. Later in the summer these washfields will be grazed by cattle or, later still, cut for hay. Wader chicks will crouch in the shadow of the sedge tussocks left by the slow-moving bullocks, while anxious parents drive off the sharp-eyed crow,

Moorhens dash for cover behind reeds at the edge of a mere.

as it too looks for food for its own chicks in the nest back in the riverside willow.

The ditches and dykes are alive with colour – water forget-me-not, yellow flag, comfrey and loosestrife – a bewildering mixture of blues and yellows, whites and purples, lining the watersides. Down in the clear depths, pondweeds and hornworts reach upwards towards the platelike leaves of fringed water lily, or the water-piercing spears of arrowhead. The plants are food and shelter to a myriad of tiny animals which give life to the ducklings, in their turn prey to the lurking jack pike. This habitat, rich in colourful wildlife and once such a common sight, is now restricted to a few remnants. You can almost count them on your fingers. Pevensey Levels and Amberley Wild Brooks in Sussex, the meadows of the Hampshire Avon and the "Ings" of the river Derwent in Yorkshire, The Nene and the Ouse Washes in Cambridgeshire and West Sedgemoor in Somerset.

Still flooded in most winters, West Sedgemoor attracts many duck together with huge flocks of waders, up to 15,000 lapwing, 10,000 dunlin and 500 golden plover as well as passage waders like whimbrel and green sandpipers and a small flock of wintering Bewick's swans. But to see wildfowl in really impressive numbers one must go back to the Ouse Washes where between 30,000 and 40,000 wigeon, up to 7000 mallard and teal with lesser numbers of pintail, shoveler, gadwall, tufted duck and pochard, coupled with over 2000 Bewick's swans, make

161

up one of the largest and most exciting assemblages of wildfowl to be seen anywhere in the United Kingdom.

At West Sedgemoor, the turf has not been underdrained or ploughed in 700 years. The spring carpet of flowers has an unsurpassable beauty; fields full of early flowering yellow kingcups give way to the whites and browns of meadow rue and sedge intermixed with the delicate pinks of the scarce green winged and southern marsh orchids and the bolder purples of meadow thistle. Waders breed in large numbers, snipe, redshank, the black-tailed godwit, and curlew, their beautiful song reminiscent of the wild open moors of the north. Herons from the nearby heronry stand motionless in the ditches waiting for unwary eels or minnows, and the mewing of buzzards is a reminder of the West Country setting for this most attractive of wetlands.

But nearly a third of the moor has now been underdrained and grows carrots and potatoes, or modern grass leys; whilst new schemes to underdrain and pump dry small blocks of pasture are constantly coming forward. In 1979 the Minister rejected the argument for retaining the established low cost farming system over 50 acres and grant-aided a drainage scheme which destroyed its ecological interest.

Year after year, more of our wetlands are drained, with government grant aid, and none outside reserves seem safe. Outside the breeding season waders – whether from British breeding grounds or from far afield – gather in numbers on the sea coast. A different sort of birdwatching presents itself. T. A. Coward (*Bird Haunts and Nature Memories*, 1922) relates an October wader-watching expedition on the Dee estuary.

High tides in early October are perhaps the best of the year from the bird-watcher's point of view, for though large numbers of northern waders arrive in September, and even in August, there are in the later month hosts of winterers added to the birds of passage. These last are here for a few days, or at the most weeks, and in winter have passed far to the south; in the warmest months they are at their breeding haunts when the short Arctic summer uncovers the luxuriant tundras. But the great southward tide of northern birds is not always regular in its visits; the shores may be lined in September and vacated in October, for the autumn crowds ebb and flow, and a poor day may be followed by one of great abundance.

The first waders which sought the still uncovered rocks which fringe the grass-grown portion of the Eye were dunlins and ringed plovers;

these and numerous noisy and very wide-awake redshanks had been feeding as long as possible upon the sand. The redshanks, always nervous, were quick to see that the islet was not untenanted; each as it approached went off yelling blue murder towards Middle Hilbre, and we were glad to see the spoilsports depart. The dunlins arrived in flocks of from a score to several hundred birds, wheeled round, flashing silvery white as they all turned their underparts towards us, swept past with a rustle as of many silken skirts, and then settled almost at our feet. Immediately some tucked their bills into their scapulars, raised one leg, and dozed; others attended to their plumage, but whether awake or, apparently, asleep, they hopped nearer and nearer as the water pushed them up the sloping rocks. The ringed plovers did not pack with the dunlins, but ran in the shallow water, snapping up the tiny shrimp-like crustaceans which came ashore with every ripple. Sanderlings, already in grey winter garments, came to joint the throng, for the love of companionship is strong in small waders; the Deeside fisherman classes all three, and any strangers such as stints, as "little birds"; they are hardly worth powder and shot, unless he can rake a crowd and pick the victims up by the dozen.

A few yards away, on the red rock, a single knot, grey-backed, black-billed and olive-legged, dozed unconcernedly, and soon some fifty or sixty of these inhabitants of the Far North, breeders in Greenland or the little known Taimyr, swept past, followed immediately by many hundreds, which, after a sharp swing, dropped on the sand, each in alighting holding its pointed wings erect for a noticeable interval. They crowded, as they always do, and ran, a little grey cloud on the ruddy sand, calling a chorus of sharp notes, *knut, knut.* Fanciful writers connected the bird which wades and runs back before the advancing waves with the tradition of Canute, but the longshore man, who named the bird before Linnæus invented *canutus*, knew more about its voice than such writers as Camden and Drayton, and perhaps had never heard of King Canute.

The little birds were soon joined by a motley band, for variation in age and season makes the turnstones a harlequin in dress; happy the man who first named them "tortoiseshell plovers." There was no weed on the rocks to be thrown over, no pebbles to be turned, so the little party rested at the edge of a sandstone ridge. With them were one or two purple sandpipers, stout little waders who find the companionship of rock hunters more to their taste than the birds which haunt the sandy shore; there are usually some of these two species on the weed-fringed rocks of Hilbre. The curlew sandpiper, a bird with a long, slightly curved bill and conspicuous white upper tail-coverts, was not present, nor was that diminutive dunlin, the little stint; the majority of these two species had no doubt passed in August or September. A few often appear amongst the Dee little birds, but they are never really common.

Curlews, easily distinguished by their size and note from the whimbrels, constantly passed in parties, their long curved bills outlined against the sky; on Middle Hilbre they gathered until, from the Eye, three-quarters of a mile away, it looked as if the grass was browsed by inumerable tiny brown sheep. They left the Eye severely alone; the curlew's sight is too sharp. Not so the pies, for when the sand-browned water lapped the red rocks below us they began to settle, first a single bird, then a score, then hundreds at a time. They saw us and were nervous, but they clung, from habit, to this high-tide roost, and though at times all rose at once and flew round the rock, the scare soon abated and peace reigned once more. Peace? No, they were hardly peaceful, for as each fresh party arrived it drove the first comers into the tide. The reefs at the Red Rocks on the Cheshire shore were one by one submerged, and party after party of pies and godwits, which had used this rest so long as the tide allowed, came swinging, with much conversation, across the water. The godwit flies with the neck drawn back, its bill held straight, but when these barking bar-tails passed the slight uptilt of the beak showed clearly. The bar-tailed godwits settled with the oyster-catchers, swelling the uneasy crowd; they leapt out of the waves, and with a flutter of wings dropped where the crowd was thickest. Thus the congested area upon the rocks, now thousands strong, was in constant unrest; birds from the outside dropped into the crush and pushed the outer members into the water, where the pies, at any rate, swam comfortably, though the bird, it is affirmed, only swims when wounded! With one lot of bar-tails, always a numerous autumn visitor to this coast, were five larger birds, standing higher on their darker legs, whose tails at once gave them away as the rarer black-tailed godwits.

Few wader notes are more beautiful than the liquid *tluie* of the grey plover, known to the local gunners as the silver plover to distinguish it from the golden and green plovers. Both these species are common on the marshes, but seldom come far seaward; the silver is the real shore bird. One or two "wings" passed, but did not settle; in winter dress as in summer the grey is one of the most beautiful of our many waders. Cormorants passed on strong wing, flying straight and with businesslike determination; they pass up to the edge of the marsh and hunt the gutters on the ebb. Away over Hilbre clouds of little birds and

The female curlew settles to brood her young.

knots, too far off to distinguish species, turned and twisted, flashing like silvery rain as they swooped suddenly down; high tide for some means rest, for others aerial recreation. Away in the main wigeon, pintail, and a few mallard drifted up on the tide, avoiding the bustling tugs which thrust their way seaward, the flowing tide curling against their straining bows; here and there a scoter, black upon the water, allowed itself to be carried upstream, but the majority of these seaducks were diving over the submerged banks in the Bay. We neither saw nor heard the geese, pink-footeds and white-fronteds, which had arrived before September ended; they were up on the marshes or the Sealand fields.

Then came a lull. The last bank of empty cockle shells was covered in the little muddy inlets, cut deep in the blue clay; the last sea-pie deserted the rocks at our feet. It was high tide, and the birds had moved to make the most of the ebb; the only avian companion left, beside the wheatear and thrush, which were sheltering somewhere out of sight, was a lively fly-catching rock pipit, who absolutely ignored our presence. We rose and looked seaward. The tide had turned, and soon the scoters came back, and odd gulls, less visible than a black duck on the glistening water, drifted past towards the Bay. A guillemot returned from an unconscious up-river trip; a line of wet glacial clay fringed the rocks, a patch of sand, a wet whaleback, hove in sight, the top of a bank; the water was receding as fast as it had come. The pies raced to each bank as it appeared, competing with the curlews and knots for the marine worms, the crustaceans, and molluscs which strove to bury themselves in the sand. The birds know that it is a race against time; they must catch these fugitives before they realise that they are stranded high and dry. The gulls and waders distributed themselves over miles and miles of freshly exposed banks; only a few redshanks now came near the islands, probing the sands. The larger gulls went seaward towards the great banks of Liverpool Bay, the common gulls and black-heads scattered over the ever widening stretch between us and the land, picking up cockles before they burrowed. These the common gulls smashed by carrying them into the air and dropping them from a height, repeating the performance time after time, until their purpose was achieved. We had a long wait until the gutters were shallow enough for us to cross, but the waiting time was not tedious; the common gulls smashing cockles, and the black-heads dancing in the shallows to bring up the retreating worms kept up our interest.

How the estuarine environment can change – from hour to hour as well as season to season. S. Bayliss-Smith went out in January (*British Waders in their Haunts*, 1950).

Seven o'clock on a dark and raw January morning, with snow, driven before a searching north-westerly wind, sweeping across the countryside, obliterating familiar landmarks and muffling the sound of my footsteps as I plodded down the coastal road and across the golf links towards the estuary – a most unpromising setting for an expedition of this kind, and yet – who knows? Today, one of the highest tides of the winter would flood the estuary. This weather should bring the birds very close, though the chances of photography were slender indeed. But first, the island must be discovered. Somewhere in the darkness a mile away across the mud flats was that low sandstone hummock which was my objective. Beyond it, over the distant mussel beds, the tide was already creeping in. There was no time to be lost if the intervening creeks were to be crossed dry-shod.

Striking out across the desolate waste of mud, I found the line of sand dunes behind me had disappeared before I had gone a hundred yards.

There was nothing for it but to press on blindly. Past and future had ceased to exist. The present was all that mattered, and the urgency of keeping my sense of direction in the confusion of swirling snow. It would be all too easy to bear off to the right or left in the first arc of a circle that would eventually lure me onwards to the edge of that "cruel crawling foam" which, as every schoolboy knows, brought Mary to her watery grave when she went to call the cattle home across these self-same sands of Dee – a chilling thought for a January dawn. Across the murky, snow-laden sky a leaden pallor was creeping, bringing with it a measure of comfort, for surely with daybreak approaching the island's shape would soon be visible. Yes, in a momentary lull in the blizzard, there was its familiar hump showing darkly against the horizon, still a quarter of a mile away and far to the left of where I had been heading, but immeasurably reassuring for all that.

He also described the attractions of May.

May can be, in many ways, the most exciting month of all. It is true that our resident waders are mostly scattered far and wide, and some already blessed with eggs, or young. But what about the northern migrants? It may be that we in this country are experiencing an early heat-wave with temperatures up in the seventies. But what about the North Lands? It is hard to realise, as we luxuriate in the warmth of a premature English summer, that the sub-polar regions where so many of the northern waders have their nesting-haunts are still in the grip of the arctic winter. These distant travellers, in obedience to the deepest instincts of their race, delay their northward passage until, with dramatic haste, the late arctic spring awakens to teeming life the insect population of those mosquito-ridden lands, and the fast-melting snows lay bare the seeds and berries that have, for the last nine months, been lying hidden there.

It is in May that many of these northern-nesting waders pass along our shores in strength. It is then that one can often see them in the full glory of their breeding dress. There is a great element of chance about the species that may be encountered, but this only adds to the fascination of the pursuit. The day may be rich in experience: it may be a total blank. But whether the birds are there or not, the setting is always delightful. One can dream away the noonday hours on an island in mid-May as profitably as anywhere else in the kingdom.

The dunlin is one of the most familiar shorebirds. Bayliss-Smith goes on to describe them.

In a stack-yard in winter one tends to assume that all the small birds foraging and twittering there are finches and sparrows. In the same way, unless there is a good reason for believing otherwise, one tends to assume that all the small waders busily dibbling out on the tidal ooze are Dunlins – which is really a tribute to this ubiquitous little wader, for it must have achieved a very satisfactorily balanced economy to be able to maintain its status and remain unquestionably the commonest and the most widely distributed of all the shore waders. Nor does it follow a stereotyped pattern either of behaviour or of physical proportions. It obtains its food in a variety of pleasing ways. It shows a catholicity of taste in its habitats that contrasts strongly with many of the more fastidious members of the wader tribe. It frequently occurs inland, and is a regular visitor to sewage farms. To assert that it is amongst the waders as the Starling is amongst passerine birds is not as uncomplimentary as it may sound, for the success of a species is best judged by its status in a changing world. Both birds have the same adaptability, the same disregard for convention, the same mutually helpful social traits, and both are marked successes in an age that is witnessing the rapid decrease of many more specialised species.

Knots are the waders of the big, dense estuarine flocks above all others. Henry Seebohm observed them closely (*A History of British Birds*, 1885).

It is an animating sight to watch a flock of these little Arctic strangers feeding on the mud-flats or sands. Perhaps the romance attaching to their breeding-grounds and still all but undiscovered eggs adds to the charm, and increases the interest in these birds. When feeding they usually keep well together, all pointing their heads in one direction, systematically searching the ground for food. The smaller birds which are scattered amongst them, and trip here and there up and down the sands, crossing and recrossing each other's tracks, are Dunlins; the Knots do not rush about in such an erratic manner. The legs are bent and the head is thrust well forward as the Knot seeks for its food. They often search quite close to the receding waves, following in their wake to pick up the various small animals cast ashore. Sometimes a solitary bird may be seen feeding, running to and fro, picking here and there, or standing preening its plumage. Large flocks often congregate on some favourite mud-bank and remain almost motionless for hours. If alarmed, the whole flock rises *en masse,* and on rapid wing scurries along just above the sands to quieter and safer quarters. Sometimes they

Knot. Very large numbers winter in the major estuaries.

wheel and turn, or fly for a little distance out to sea, and perform various graceful evolutions ere alighting.

Ronald Lockley (*Shearwaters*, 1942) discussed bird flight, of relevance to the near-incredible performances of wader flocks.

The flight of bird flocks has excited the curiosity of many observers. One author has said:

Their incredibly swift flight-movements are controlled by a mass-sensitiveness of visual perception, and drilled into a remarkable cohesion of flight-order by ages of immediate obedience to flock laws, with some element of physical or mental telepathy – probably of a sensitised physical nature, as yet not understood.

I asked my wife to read this explanation carefully aloud, and to tell me what it meant. My wife, who is a sensible woman, said the explanation seemed to lie in the first six and the last two words.

Bannerman includes much of interest in his essay about the oystercatcher, in *The Birds of the British Isles* (1956). It has none of the attractions of the small sandpipers for the identification expert, nor any of the romantic association with remote and

169

difficult places for the nester who enjoys the challenge of a wild and problematical bird. The oystercatcher, however, has a quality all its own – both in its breeding sites and in winter.

To watch a big flock of oystercatchers as the tide comes in, driving the birds closer together and perhaps causing them to take refuge on an exposed spit of sand not yet covered by the waves, is always an absorbing sight. Kenneth Williamson, in a short article on "Flocking Behaviour of Oystercatchers", has drawn attention to the "sham sleeping" in which the birds indulge – that is, standing quietly on one or both legs, their heads turned and bills pushed into the scapular feathers in the normal posture of resting birds, but *with the eyes wide open*. Observation of these pseudo-sleeping birds prompted the suggestion that this behaviour is related to each bird's need to maintain a clear space in its immediate neighbourhood – a vital necessity for a quick and unimpeded take-off should danger suddenly threaten the flock. Often too when a big flock is feeding on exposed sand or mud the birds keep their distance from one another but in that case the urge is more likely to be connected with an individual bird's anxiety to keep for itself any dainty morsel which it may extricate, and not have it "pinched" by a neighbour.

On one occasion in Balcary Bay, Kirkcudbrightshire, my wife and I witnessed an extraordinary performance on the part of many oystercatchers which we have never seen before or since. The month was October (1951), the tide was out, and a wide expanse of sands lay exposed. Oystercatchers were spread all over the bay and all were running hither and thither with quick little steps as if engrossed in a game. Watching through binoculars we saw that the birds were collecting cockle shells and placing them in little heaps. Each bird was making its own little pile to which it ran with a new shell with a quick furtive run. Not one, but every bird was so engaged, and all over the sandy bay the little piles were growing larger. We watched for an hour before having to leave and could not even guess the reason or object of this curious operation.

We have on more than one occasion seen oystercatchers doing a sort of dance – invariably on the edge of the tide. One bird among a considerable gathering of stationary birds will suddenly start hopping up and down, then gradually the whole flock will follow suit until all the birds have joined in, whether on one leg or two it was difficult to make out. We have seen a single bird do this on the edge of an incoming tide, but when a whole crowd are so engaged the effect is most comical.

The reason seems obscure, but the performance is certainly catching.

E. A. Armstrong loved oystercatchers. He wrote of them in *Birds of the Grey Wind* (1940).

On the eastern shore of Strangford there is a small humpbacked island. The landward side provides a sheltered sanctuary for goodly trees, which, in their turn, protect a farmhouse from the bitter winds. Within twenty feet of the tide snuggles a tiny shieling in which I stay now and again. It serves my purpose better than a tent, for the birds are accustomed to it and I need not spend much time settling in.

To arrive there from town is to make a transition so abrupt and complete that on every visit I am a little bemused that such a sudden change of surroundings – and accompanying mood – should be possible. The first evening I spent in this peaceful place remains vivid in my memory. The world seemed molten gold as the sun drew near the horizon. The long-drawn fluting of the curlew mingled with the redshank's sharp whistling, and the thrushes sang as if they saw the gates of heaven opening. Two swans caught in a rosy beam far out amongst the slakes looked like squatting flamingoes; and when a kestrel flew swiftly past, hovered for a few moments over the shore and disappeared, the departure of the little hunter made the stillness and peacefulness of the place more emphatic ... I went to bed content. The tranquillity of that lovely scene saturated the depths of my being – and still lingers there to-day.

Oystercatchers – splendidly attractive and excitable birds.

I do not often sleep soundly during a first night in unfamiliar surroundings. So it was on this occasion; my wakeful moments were seasons of delight by reason of a sweet twittering heard rising above the murmur of the sea. It was like an excited musical dispute, suddenly breaking forth and almost as quickly appeased. The staccato cries became more rapid and the chorus faded in an accelerating diminuendo. One might imagine each of a party of birds trying to make his opinions heard above the voices of the others. Had some careless individual disturbed the slumbers of his companions? It was an intriguing sound, a reminder of a world full of life just outside one's door, strange and unexplored. I knew that the birds were sea-pies and that they were up to some of their numerous and puzzling tricks: idly speculating as to the meaning of the musical commotion I soon fell asleep. Years later when I listened at night to the wood-rails (*Aramides cajanea cajanea*) piping in chorus by a lagoon-shore in the Central American jungle I was reminded of the oystercatchers, and a wave of homesickness swept over me as I recalled Strangford Lough and its pied pipers.

These odd birds, as we shall presently see, have many other strange habits besides that of holding nocturnal colloquies; moreover the Celtic imagination has woven them into myth and legend so that the charm of their odd manners is augmented by a multitude of pleasant associations. The most familiar folk-tale concerning them explains the origin of the bird's black and white plumage.

At ebb-tide the Saviour rested by the shore, sad and weary, and not far from the fringe of His robe a bird with a long bill picked and probed in the sea-wrack, seeking small shell-fish. The sea-pie, however, was as vigilant as ever, and when he spied fierce men approaching down the glen he piped a warning call. But neither by sea nor by land was there a way of escape and the Lord Jesus sat there to await the coming of His enemies. With shrill cries the bird besought Him, saying: "Yonder they come to take Thee, my Lord; make haste to hide." Seizing great strings of sea-tangle he laid them upon Him and worked with such diligence that when the wicked company drew near there was nought to be seen but rocks and wrack with a red-eyed bird screaming along the shore. So they hurried on to seek Him elsewhere.

Saint Michael was for arraying the bird in white like an angel as a reward for the love he bore the Saviour, but Saint Brigit, the foster-mother of Christ, would not have it so, and said: "Let the bird that saved my Child be as he ever was save for a touch of whiteness about him, for remembrance." And so it is that the Breedyeen, Bride's birdikin, carries his red bill still and is clothed in black, but when he flies he shows the white cross which was given him from Heaven. And since, as the Holy Fathers say, Saint Bride is the Blessed Virgin born again amongst the Celtic folk to care for the weans, her bird watches over little children that they may come to no harm. On her day, the 1st of February, the birds, it is said, begin to build their nests; and country folk in the North of Ireland honour her by plaiting rushes into crosses and hanging them up in the houses and over the doors to bring a blessing on the home and cattle. I remember as a lad sitting with an old man on the shore at Ballycastle, over against Rathlin, and being shown how to plait these emblems – probably originally symbols of the sun.

If I had to describe the oystercatcher to some one not familiar with his appearance I should be inclined to say: "Look out for a stump-tailed shore magpie with a long red nose." He is rather a swaggering, Micawberish fellow and his eccentric tastes are in keeping with his odd garb. He will stand plethorically on a rock, hardly moving, for long periods; but at other times, as we shall see, he is as gay and sprightly as a pie of the woods.

"Oystercatcher" is not an apt title. Dr J. M. Dewar, indeed, has investigated the American bird's habits and shown that it can and does eat oysters. According to him the reason why the modern oystercatcher does not catch many oysters is that the oysters in their wisdom have retreated out of reach! So far as the British Isles are concerned either of the two popular names, mussel-picker or sea-pie is more appropriate.

Many are the artifices of the bird in securing his prey. He will prowl about the mussel-banks prising open the shells by the dorsal or ventral surface, or probe in the sand for molluscs and other organisms. Or you may see him running about the rocks scrutinizing the limpets and neatly turning over any which are not tightly clamped in place. More often the birds spend their time searching for food amongst the seaweed. On the Dutch islands where they nest far from any water other than small canals and ditches they feed in the fields as curlews sometimes do in England.

Most of the larger islets of Strangford Lough harbour a pair of nesting oystercatchers. On one of these I had a peculiar experience. I spent about an hour in a hiding-tent photographing terns, and when I came out pottered about for a further three-quarters of an hour, looking for nests and young birds, until my friend rowed back from a neighbouring island. All the time a pair of oystercatchers had been flying about, calling shrilly. We settled down on a sunny bank a dozen yards from the sea to sun-bathe and have some lunch. It was very pleasant reclining languidly amidst the quivering, silvery-pink pom-poms of the thrift, looking over the sea to the mauve, tower-crowned hill of Scrabo. Terns were fishing daintily, a pair of great black-backed gulls snarled overhead, and a rock pipit fluttering over the whispering grass uttered, now and then, a sweet half-hearted trill. After we had been there for some time I noticed, and drew my friend's attention to, a reddish object in the floating seaweed close to a rounded black stone, just awash. As I remarked to him, it looked a little like an oystercatcher crouching in the water; but that this could actually be the case seemed so absurd that we dismissed the matter from our minds, and continued our leisurely meal. Suddenly my companion said: "Look at the oystercatcher walking out of the water!" The object that we had seen in the sea had disappeared and a bedraggled bundle of black and white feathers was dejectedly picking its slow way up the beach. It was obvious that throughout two hours or longer the bird had "frozen" - in two senses - in the water. Hearing the parents' warning notes it had cowered, all but submerged, where it had been feeding. I decided that a photograph of the oystercatcher would be of interest and stripped off my clothes ready to swim after it, if necessary. But it had evidently had enough of the water and allowed me to catch it with ease. The incident illustrates the blind, automatic character of the responses of a young bird.

Another example of a common wader is the lapwing. Edmund Selous appreciated them (*Bird Life Glimpses*, 1905).

Of all the birds that we have here, the peewits, for a great part of the year, give most life to the barren lands. In the winter, as I say, they disappear entirely, going off to the fens, though, here and there, their voice remains, mimicked, to the life, by a starling. In February, however, they return, and are soon sporting, and throwing their fastastic somersaults, over their old, loved breeding-grounds. Pleasant it is to have this breezy joy of spring-time, once again, to have the accustomed tilts and turns and falls and rushing sweeps, before one's eyes, and the old calls and cries in one's ears - the sound of the wings, too, free as the wild air they beat, and sunlight glints on green and white, and silver-flying snowflakes. "What a piece of work is a *peewit*!" The glossy green of the upper surface - smooth and shining as the shards of a beetle - glows, in places, with purple burnishings, and, especially, on each shoulder there is an intensified patch, the last bright twin-touch of adornment. The pure, shining white of the neck and ventral surface - shining almost into silver as it catches the sun - is boldly and beautifully contrasted with the black of the throat, chin, and forehead. The neat little, corally stilt-legs are an elegant support for so much beauty, and the crest that crowns it is as the fringe to the scarf, or the tassel to the fez. There is, besides, the walk, pose, poise, and easy swing of the whole body.

A familiar species already mentioned is the redshank. Bannerman describes it thus in *The Birds of the British Isles* (1956).

The redshank must rank close to the curlew as our most familiar wading bird. It is, indeed, the very spirit of the marshes – a noisy restless creature as it has been proclaimed – but nonetheless a bird which we associate instinctively with the wide open spaces of our coasts: tidal estuaries, marram-covered marshes, mud-flats, sandy and rocky shores, all are brought to mind in turn. In the breeding season we find the redshank far inland, making its well-concealed nest in tussocky grass, sometimes 1000 to 1500 feet above the sea, while it may equally be sought in lowland localities as on the bonnie banks of Loch Lomond, where Robert Gray discovered a colony in a grassy park, close on 100 years ago. When the water fell low in the loch the redshanks would choose the line of highwater mark for their breeding place, the so-called "nests", placed on the mass of sticks and straws blown on shore by the

The noisy redshank is soberly coloured, but quite dramatic in flight.

wind. South of the Border the Norfolk Broads attract the redshanks in numbers, especially when flooding is rife, or we may find it by some secluded lake or by the banks of a slow-moving stream winding its way through the meadowland. The redshank's choice of habitat is almost as varied as its choice of a nesting site. Being with us both in winter and summer, its clamorous voice is to be heard at all seasons, and many a shore-shooter has had cause to curse the redshank's vigilance when attempting to stalk geese or wild duck before daylight has dawned. The warning cry rings out and every bird within miles is instantly on the alert – or more likely on the wing.

The redshank is just one of many elements which made Strangford Lough in winter so attractive to E. A. Armstrong (*Birds of the Grey Wind*, 1940).

The long lights of evening in the desert, like those of our wintry loughs, are not beautiful merely by contrast with the torrid heat of noonday or the full summer sunshine; they etch the outlines of hills and rocks, mass the shadows, and quicken into vivid luminosity every detail in the foreground. Thus, on fine days in winter when the air is still, the sky clear above the lough, and mellow light floods the wide scene, it is not less beautiful than in spring. Indeed, a peacefulness pervades the place which one can never experience when birds are singing, sap is rising and the animate world is writhing in the frenzy of vernal ardour. The lough is a luminous water-colour of heroic dimensions, a saga in light; land and water become subsidiary and incidental, handmaids to a greater glory. Ireland's charm, indeed, whether in winter or summer, on moorland or shore, consists in no small degree in the spaciousness of her skies, her lovely clouds, opalescent distances, and the soft, clear radiance of every remote view. The writer who describes Ireland without emphasis on the tender clarity of the light which suffuses her countryside has failed to discern one of her chief beauties.

In winter, birds which are almost indistinguishable brown specks on the mud when the summer sun is overhead are now picked out by the slanting rays with every hue accentuated. On the wing the redshank is a sylph in silver feathers, and when she alights, her legs of sealing-wax red contrast with the snowy breast to give her a very spruce appearance. The oystercatcher's pied plumage, red bill, and bright pink legs look more appropriate to the tropics than Irish foreshores. Even the demure and dumpy ringed plovers tripping along the mud in fits and starts, with yellow legs twinkling beneath dark bibs, look almost elegant. The very curlews, clear-cut against the shimmering water, possess the dignity of ibises; and the rooks as they scavenge amongst the long wreaths of sea-weed might be clad in plates of burnished purple mail.

Seebohm gave his typically close attention to another familiar wader, the ringed plover (*A History of British Birds*, 1885).

The Ringed Plover is a wild wary bird when feeding, especially in its winter-quarters, or where it has been much molested; but at its breeding-grounds it changes its character and becomes an unobstrusive little creature, by no means shy or wary, allowing you to walk within a few yards of it without betraying any signs of fear. As you approach, it often runs a little distance, then may pause to watch you with just a trace of anxiety; or more probably it flies smoothly along just above the sands, uttering a plaintive note as it goes, and alights on a little eminence to watch your movements. Few shore-birds are more engaging in their actions than the Ringed Plover. It is a pretty sight to watch half a dozen of these little creatures tripping over the sands or running amongst the pebbles and other shore débris searching for food. They run with great swiftness, every now and then pausing a moment, then darting on a few feet, then resting again, putting the observer irresistibly in mind of the progress of a fly on a window-pane. They keep close to the edge of the water, following the receding waves to pick up their meal, often wading through little pools, ever being driven backwards by the approaching waves, and as constantly following them as they recede, to glean the rich harvest of marine animals left by the receding tide. If the shore is sandy the birds are easily discernible for a considerable distance; but when it is strewn with pebbles and shingle it is hard to discover their whereabouts, and very often they keep rising almost at the intruder's feet, squatting close until almost trodden upon ere they take wing. The flight of this little bird is performed by regular and quick beatings of the wings, and every now and then it glides for a short distance, especially when going to alight. They usually fly quite close to the ground, sometimes not more than a few inches above it, but at other times they may be seen to soar high in the air and fly round and round; they often do this if shot at or otherwise alarmed. When in flocks they sometimes perform various graceful evolutions in the air, wheeling round, simultaneously turning or swooping close to the ground and rising again as if all were moved by one common impulse. When engaged in searching for food the Ringed Plovers occasionally mix with other shore-birds, such as Dunlins or other Sandpipers; but when

177

disturbed they generally keep to themselves, flying away in a compact flock like Starlings.

The turnstone is somewhat different in its behaviour. Bannerman described the bird well in *The Birds of the British Isles* (1956).

The turnstone has been described as certainly among the most engaging, and perhaps the most confiding of all our shore-birds, and must be known to all who have an interest in the bird-life of our coast. It is seldom seen alone; more often little parties of eight or more will be found together, nimbly running over the rocks or maybe resting contentedly on some reef or promontory within close approach of the waves. Among the sea-wrack and pebbles polished smooth by the action of the water, the turnstones in their winter dress are well camouflaged, and since they are more easily approached than many of our wading birds one may come upon them unaware of their presence until the little flock take wing with what T. A. Coward described as a short redpoll-like trill, showing the white rump and the bar on the wing. Even the orange legs are inconspicuous among the yellow seaweed, but when the birds are perched high on some rock the brilliance of their legs is apparent and very striking. On muddy shores, where the birds feed with ringed plover, purple sandpipers, knots, and curlews, the turnstones are not difficult to recognize: even in such varied company they keep very much to themselves and should anything disturb them all will take wing simultaneously, flying perhaps a short distance before alighting.

One observation of turnstones gave rise to one of the most famous of all short notes in a bird journal: 'Turnstones feeding on human corpse'! Often with turnstones may be found purple sandpipers. H. M. S. Blair, in Bannerman's book, gives the old-style collector's view of this species, finishing with a line which would hardly find its way into a present-day guide!

Every sportsman and naturalist who has encountered the purple sandpiper will endorse its claim to be regarded as the tamest of the waders. It runs fearlessly about within a few feet of the intruder, and people gathering mussels or the like often find themselves attended by one or two "tankers" ready to pick up any discarded fragments of the shellfish. A party of a dozen or so of these birds has been known to settle around a gunner awaiting the evening flight, and even to approach to within a few inches of his face as he lay on the weed. Indeed, it often proves difficult to alarm the purple sandpiper into taking wing; "provokingly so, now and then, when on wishes to obtain a specimen, and the bird, refusing to rise, stands quietly with its head upon one side, as though it were highly amused" (Saxby). That so confiding a bird should take up its quarters about docks and harbours, as it frequently does, is hardly surprising.

Purple sandpipers swim well, if slowly, and are more often seen afloat than most waders. Stevenson refers to several seen by a Mr Wells "dipping suddenly under water with a plunge, so much resembling that of the water rat, that when Mr Wells first saw one of these birds perform this action, he actually mistook it for a water rat". Normally these sandpipers dive only if hard hit and winged.

Collingwood Ingram (*In Search of Birds*, 1966) included his views on egg-collecting in a passage about one of the most attractive and unusual of all waders, the red-necked phalarope.

Of all the world's waders the little Red-necked Phalarope is, perhaps, the most adorable. This is not only because of its graceful movements and the ladylike elegance of its form so prettily clad in grey, sepia and white with a happy touch of red on the neck, but chiefly because of the

A tiny bird to winter at sea – the red-necked phalarope.

bird's charmingly trustful nature. Indeed, if one can judge from its behaviour, the Red-necked Phalarope must regard man as a creature no more to be feared than a browsing beast. For instance, I have seen a male – for it is only that sex which attends to the bird's domestic duties – fly confidently straight towards me, alight close by and then walk calmly on to its nest, hardly more than a yard from where I was standing. This implicit faith in the harmlessness of human beings must at times have cost the species dear, for its eggs have always been greatly sought after by unscrupulous oölogists, many of whom would travel far and shamelessly flout the law in order to add a British taken clutch – for an identical one from the Continent will not satisfy their cupidity – to their collections.

As I have said in another book the ethics of egg-collecting should present no problem. If a British species be sufficiently rare to make its eggs worth acquiring, then in my opinion they should very decidedly not be taken; if, on the other hand, a bird is so common that its status is not likely to be endangered by the loss of a few clutches then, surely, there can be no point in collecting its eggs. Upon what grounds, therefore, can the oölogist justify his occupation? Perhaps I am unduly prejudiced against the egg collector for my interests have always been centred on the living nestling and never on the inanimate shell from which, if left to nature, that nestling would have emerged.

But in the little island of which I speak blame for the recent deplorable reduction in the numbers of phalaropes cannot, I think, be wholly laid at the door of those misguided enthusiasts. I believe that their decrease is largely, if not mainly, due to the practice prevailing among the local crofters of tethering their cows near the small sheets of water inhabited by the birds – namely, just where they are most likely to site their nests. If the animals do not themselves destroy the eggs by treading on them, the ropes by which they are attached, dragging heavily over the ground, are almost bound to do so.

Perhaps the most interesting thing about the Red-necked Phalarope is its singular, and, among British birds, unique breeding habits. Once the eggs have been laid the female takes no further part in the proceedings and thereafter the duties of incubation and the rearing of the young devolve solely upon the male. Although polyandry has never been recorded in this species, it seemed to me rather strange that during my first visit I saw only one female to four males – the nests of three of which I succeeded in locating. Admittedly since incubation had by then started, the females, having ceased to take an active interest in their family affairs, may well have already left the island.

Many waders occur in Britain principally as passage migrants; they neither breed nor spend the winter here. This lends all the more interest in the diverse places which they do inhabit at other times. The wood sandpiper is an example. Here is a passage from Bannerman's *The Birds of the British Isles* (1956).

It should be noted that despite its name it [the wood sandpiper] is not a woodland bird. In its winter quarters in tropical Africa it must normally be sought wherever there are pools of fresh water in the interior; even in the dry thornscrub belt it occurs wherever the remnants of a stream have been left. Its favourite places in West Africa (Mali and Niger) are the stagnant pools in the semi-arid belt, all that is left, after the long drought, of the once flowing streams; here gather the insects upon which it thrives. Notes sent to me by many correspondents in West Africa stated that it is seen in little parties more often than singly, but that odd birds are occasionally encountered. Sometimes it may be observed on the branches of a tree like a common sandpiper. In its winter habitat it is usually fairly tame, allowing close approach when it is engaged in its search for spiders, insects, worms, molluscs, and various larvae which constitute its food in such surroundings. It has been known to take very small fish on the salt marshes of Bahrain Island in the Persian Gulf, while in Britain Colonel J. K. Standford dissected a bird which had been feeding on beetles and may-flies besides other insects. Stanford observed that when feeding the sandpiper holds the bill under water and sweeps it from side to side in the manner of an avocet; but whether this method is commonly used is not certain, for no one else appears to have remarked it. Dr William Serle, who was able to study the wood sandpiper in its winter quarters in northern Nigeria, told me that with the exception of the common sandpiper it was the most numerous sandpiper in Sokoto and around Zaria. In the dry season they generally occurred singly or in twos and threes, and frequented the pools on the river beds or the few remaining tabkis or marshes; they seemed to become more numerous on the marshes in the middle of July and then their habits changed, for throughout the rest of July and August they were to be seen in smaller or larger flocks, often consorting with other waders such as the black-tailed godwit. About this time they were observed feeding gregariously in the marsh, or flying over their feeding grounds, wheeling and packing like a flock of dunlin.

In the (ex-Belgian) Congo, where the wood sandpiper may be found in savanna and forest country alike, it is reported by Dr Chapin to be a

The attractive wood sandpiper is a small, northerly breeding wader.

rather common bird along the rivers from September to March, and records show that it may even be seen at that latitude in August. It winters throughout the whole country except in the very high mountains. Nevertheless Rockfeller and Murphy obtained one at 7050 feet in Marungu and others have been collected at slightly lower elevations north-east of the Kivu volcanoes. Dr Chapin adds that in the Congo the wood sandpiper is not particularly fond of woods but is found usually in open or grassy spots near marshes and water-courses, or on bars in rivers at low water.

In very different surroundings on the other side of Africa Sir Geoffrey Archer found wood sandpipers fairly plentifully distributed in Abyssinia, where they haunt the marshy places and the grassy banks of streams in the high moorland country at 8000–10,000 feet altitude, or the edges of open sheets of water such as Lakes Abaya and Haramaia. Generally in such places two or three birds are to be seen together, though sometimes a small party may be flushed.

The green sandpiper is closely related to the wood sandpiper and looks very similar to it. In Bannerman's book, J. H. McNeile detailed the breeding haunts in Estonia.

Between 1935 and 1938 I was fortunate enough to see over thirty clutches of green sandpiper in Estonia, west of Tartu. The pairs were scattered over a considerable area of flat swampy forest of spruce, birch, and poplar, and laid their eggs in nests of jay, song-thrush, or mistle-thrush, or else in an old squirrel's drey. The larger nests were most often chosen, but many of them were so old and flattened that it was difficult to know whether they had originally been built by jays or squirrels. One of the thrush nests, obviously a new one which had been taken for their own use by the sandpipers, had only a grass lining still, and might have been a redwing's.

The green sandpipers were unobtrusive while they had eggs; one could go for hours without being aware that the birds were about, until a bird was disturbed from a ditch, or was heard calling. Nests in which they elected to lay their eggs varied in height from sixty feet or more (right in the top of a good-sized spruce) down to a bare three feet, where the sandpipers had annexed an absolutely new song-thrush's nest low down in a juniper bush and built partly on a rough wooden fence separating the forest from a cultivated field. The bird sitting on these four fresh eggs was astonishingly bold, for after allowing me to photograph it on the nest at close range, it stood up in the nest and pecked my fingers when I attempted to lift it off the eggs.

This was an extreme case, of course, but quite often the sitting bird would only leave its eggs when one had climbed up almost within touching distance of the nest. In other cases, on the other hand, the eggs were only discovered by climbing up to the nest on the off-chance, the sitting *ochropus* having slipped off quietly just ahead of one. When the eggs were in *Turdus* nests, the sitting sandpiper's beak could sometimes be seen from the ground below, sticking out over the edge of the nest.

When disturbed from its eggs, the green sandpipers often flew away silently, but sometimes they circled round uttering a rather green-shank-like alarm-call.

As soon as their eggs were hatched, however, their behaviour changed completely when disturbed; they flew round in a fever of agitation and excitement, perching at intervals on top of some small tree, and raising their wings with incessant cries of alarm.

Moving to the far north, the activities of the old collectors, with a good deal of new discoveries being made and challenges met, make good reading. H. J. Pearson in *Three Summers amongst the Birds of Russian Lapland* (1904) wrote of his exploits.

June 22nd. – As all our efforts to find a nest of the Bar-tailed Godwit at Pulozero had failed, we decided to go to Raz-Navolok to-day and see if the species was breeding there. The distance from the head of Lake Pulozero to Lake Kolozero is said to be four versts, but it took us quite an hour, walking at a rate of nearly four miles an hour. I found the latter lake was 60 feet above the former by aneroid. Leaving Pulozero at 1.40 p.m., we started on Kolozero at 2.50 and traversed the fifteen versts to the head of the lake in two and a half hours, sailing part of the way. Then came another tramp over the short verst which divides Kolozero from Lake Pereyaver and forms the watershed between the Arctic Ocean and the White Sea. We were glad to find that Mr. Witherby's flies had not yet appeared on the scene, nor did we meet with them on our return. Pereyaver is the Lapp, and Permosozero the Russian name of the lake, while Rae gives it as Pieresozero. We started on this lake at 6 p.m., and assisted by a good breeze most of the way, completed the twelve versts at 8.10 p.m., and then stopped for a meal. A good dry path across the next portage made its four versts appear short ones. Just before reaching Lake Imandra, Juno put up something a few yards from the path, and rushed off after it; then returned to assist in the search and "set" a Capercaillie's nest with seven eggs nearly ready for hatching. The nest was on rather damp ground and thinly covered with juniper scrub.

There is a good hut at the head of Lake Imandra where the river Kurenga (Koro: Rae) enters it from Lake Pereyaver; and good fishing also we heard, confirmed by a small Lapp camp with nets and boats a little lower down. A bitterly cold north-east wind, which brought several heavy showers of rain, took us rapidly over the fifteen versts of water to Rax-Navolok, where we arrived at 1 a.m., starved through. The station consisted of one wooden hut, and two small turf. I find it difficult to select an English name which will convey any idea of these human residences. As I opened the door of the hut, a puff of air met me which seemed quite strong enough to take a wasp nest. A man and his wife were asleep on a wooden bed in one corner, and a young man on another in the opposite one. However wind and rain clearly showed we must join the party. All got up at once to welcome us, and made a good fire which cleared the atmosphere a little – most important item – restored us to a reasonable degree of warmth, and cooked our supper. I counted twelve people in that hut whilst we were eating. At last some of them cleared out and we fixed our hammocks up, but the fame of these new beds spread, and we had an admiring audience of four women besides men to see us in them. Finally the man and woman returned to their bed, two of our men joined the young man in his, and we swung between them.

June 23rd. – Our Russian had lived at Raz-Navolok for some time as one of the station hands before he was employed on the telegraph, so he

Bar-tailed (left) and black-tailed godwits – long-billed shore birds.

knew the country. He took us over a well-marked path to the winter station which lies some little distance from Lake Imandra. This is a place of much greater importance than the summer one, and consists of a church, three large houses of two storeys, and a number of Lapp huts, many of the last much decayed. The three houses have been erected by Government for the use of the seamen on their annual journeys north and south. These men leave their ships in the fjords on the northern coasts of the country, and sledge overland to their homes in the towns round the White Sea, to spend the winter with their families. They return north to their ships in March, and are thus able to get to sea about two months earlier than if they waited for the ice in the White Sea to break up. At the time of our visit the whole place was uninhabited.

A large marshy tract extends for nearly a mile from these houses to the lake below. Birds were numerous here, Wood-Sandpipers, Whimbrel, Golden Plover, Greenshanks, &c., objecting strongly to our disturbing them; but we had travelled over more than half its length before we heard the note of the bird we had come for. A male Bar-tailed Godwit, in his handsome breeding plumage, was sitting on a pine-tree, giving out loud angry notes. I shall not attempt to reproduce them, because most of the efforts to print intelligibly the notes of birds have appeared to me such dismal failures I prefer not to join the band of interpreters. This bird behaved very differently to those we had seen at Maselsid, and it was at once quite clear that he was part owner in a nest not far off; but where? We tried for some time to discover what particular section of the marsh he was most interested in; this failed utterly, partly through preconceived ideas of what his behaviour ought to be. Then Musters devoted himself to watching that bird, while I took a part of the marsh I thought the most likely to contain the nest, and searched it yard by yard, and our two men wandered hopelessly about. After this had gone on for an hour and a half the Russian went off into the wood near; and on his return, as he emerged from the fringe of small trees forming the edge of the wood, he nearly stepped on the hen bird, which rose with cries even louder and more angry than those of the male, from four young, hatched certainly within the last twelve hours, for the remains of the egg shells still lay in the nest. And we had come for eggs, not young in down. If that was not a trying moment to the temper, I leave fellow-ornithologists to imagine one!

The other man had been within a few yards of the nest, but the female had not stirred. When we knew its position we were able to trace the action of the male during the whole time we had been on the ground, and found it corresponded very closely with that usually taken by the male Black-tailed Godwit under similar circumstances. A few pines – chiefly dead – were scattered over the area where we first disturbed him, and he perched on these, screaming loudly, until the man went near the nest, when he came down to the ground and redoubled his cries; on several occasions he flew towards the nest in front of the men. In fact, if we had only understood his procedure, he completely "gave the show away," behaviour very different to that of the Greenshank and Spotted Redshank. Of course this was probably due to our having disturbed the pair during the interesting period when the young had just been hatched; and it is absurd to deduce general rules from one pair of birds. Still I think it will be found that the two species of Godwit act very similarly when they have a nest; and those accustomed to the ways of the Black-tailed will have little difficulty in locating the nest of the Bar-tailed species.

One of the young was still in the nest when I arrived at the spot; we caught the other three a few yards off after considerable trouble, and replaced them in the nest, but it was impossible to kept them quiet until Musters shot the old birds.

The nest was placed on a hummock of green moss, and was of a deep saucer-shape, deeper than a Whimbrel's. It was lined with lichen and dried moss. A little scrub gave the sitting bird partial shelter. The legs of the young birds were a wigeon-grey colour, and those of the old birds nearly black. Neither of the old birds had any incubation spots.

On our return to the station at night a telegraph official, passing through to Kandalax, immediately recognised the bird, gave its Russian name, and said it was found in dry marshes. No other native knew it, all called it a Whimbrel.

And this was all we saw of the Bar-tailed Godwit at Raz-Navolok!

Much has changed since the days of the collector. There is still more than enough left to discover, and the keen amateur can still play a great part in progressing ornithological knowledge. Birds are still the most accessible and enjoyable of the higher forms of animal life to which we humans can escape. They are, too, superb indicators of the state of the environment, and if things are going wrong for them it is a fair bet that, sooner or later, we will face problems too. The emphasis has moved to conservation and protection, rather than simply collection and establishing basic knowledge of their life history (but even this is far from complete for many of them). Long may bird study continue to stimulate birdwatching authors!

BIBLIOGRAPHY

E. A. Armstrong, *Birds of the Grey Wind*, Oxford University Press 1940

Robert Atkinson, *Quest for the Griffon*, Heinemann 1938

D. A. Bannerman, *The Birds of the British Isles*, Oliver & Boyd, Edinburgh 1956

S. Bayliss-Smith, *British Waders in their Haunts*, G. Bell & Sons, London 1950

A. W. Boyd, *The Country Diary of a Cheshire Man*, Collins 1946

Leslie Brown, *Eagles*, Michael Joseph 1955

A. Chapman, *Bird Life of the Borders*, Gurney & Jackson, London 1907

T. A. Coward, *Bird Haunts and Nature Memories*, Frederick Warne & Co. 1922

T. A. Coward, *The Birds of the British Isles and their Eggs*, Frederick Warne & Co. 1969

Frank Fraser Darling, *Island Years*, G. Bell & Sons Ltd, London 1940

John Day, *RSPB Nature Reserves*, RSPB 1983

James Fisher, *The Fulmar*, Collins 1952

James Fisher and R. M. Lockley, *Seabirds*, Collins 1954

Derek Goodwin, *Birds of Man's World*, Cornell University Press, New York 1978

Seton Gordon, *Days with the Golden Eagle*, Williams & Norgate Ltd, London 1927

Seton Gordon, *In Search of Northern Birds*, Eyre & Spottiswoode, London 1941

J. A. Harvie-Brown & T. E. Buckley, *A Fauna of the Outer Hebrides*, T. & A. Constable for David Douglas, Edinburgh 1888

Francis Heatherley, *The Peregrine Falcon at the Eyrie*, Country Life 1913

Len Howard, *Birds as Individuals*, Collins 1952

W. H. Hudson, *The Land's End*, 1908

Julian Huxley, *Bird-watching and Bird Behaviour*, Dennis Dobson 1950

Collingwood Ingram, *In Search of Birds*, Witherby & Co. 1966

Kelsall & Munn, *The Birds of Hampshire and the Isle of Wight*, 1905

R. M. Lockley, *I Know an Island*, Harrap & Co., London 1938

R. M. Lockley, *Shearwaters*, J. M. Dent & Sons 1942

R. M. Lockley, *Puffins*, J. M. Dent & Sons 1953

G. & A. Marples, *Sea Terns or Sea Swallows*, Country Life 1934

Guy Mountfort, *Portrait of a Wilderness*, Hutchinson 1958

William Macgillivray, *Rapacious Birds of Great Britain*, MacLachlan & Stewart, Edinburgh 1836

Richard Meinertzhagen, *Pirates and Predators*, Oliver & Boyd 1959

Bryan Nelson, *The Gannet*, T. & A. D. Poyser 1978

Henry J. Pearson, *Three Summers among the Birds of Russian Lapland*, R. H. Porter, London 1904

C. E. Raven, *Bird Haunts and Bird Behaviour*, Martin Hopkinson Ltd 1929

Kenneth Richmond, *Wild Venture*, Geoffrey Bles 1958

Peter Scott, *The Eye of the Wind*, Hodder & Stoughton 1977

Henry Seebohm, *A History of British Birds*, R. H. Porter 1885

Edmund Selous, *Bird Life Glimpses*, George Allen, London 1905

Edmund Selous, *The Birdwatcher in the Shetlands*, J. M. Dent 1905

John Walpole-Bond, *Field Studies of some Rarer British Birds*, Witherby & Co. 1914

John Walpole-Bond, *A History of Sussex Birds*, Witherby & Co. 1938

Kenneth Williamson, *The Atlantic Islands*, Collins 1948

G. K. Yeates, *A Bird Lover's Britain*, Philip Allan, London 1937

G. K. Yeates, *Bird Life in Two Deltas*, Faber & Faber, undated

INDEX

Figures in italics refer to page numbers of illustrations.